DAMAGED GOODS

TO

GOD'S RESTORED

TREASURE

BY

Dianne M. Dobson

Copyright © 2016 Dianne M. Dobson

All rights reserved. D.I. Publishing ,LLC   ISBN: 0-9984556-0-1

i

DEDICATION

This book is dedicated to everyone that has been sexually abused and lived with the damaging effects that your traumatic experience has caused. I pray that you will see yourself in my story and receive the healing and restoration that you've been longing for since your sexual abuse occurred. Beautiful Soul, there's hope! I love you and understand what you've been through. Today I pray that your pain and agony will end and you will see yourself in a different light.

CONTENTS

Introduction

You are not alone! Many of us feel and have felt alone and may be afraid to speak about our sexual abuse with our friends and family. We are fearful of what they would think of us, but you are not alone. According to **www.rainn.org**, one in six women become a victim of sexual abuse. The ages of women to most likely be victimized are between eighteen and thirty-four. Therefore, ladies you are not alone. This has probably happened to someone that you know and they too, may be afraid to let anyone know that they have been sexually abused. Unfortunately this happens too often and we endure this experience in solitude, confined by the horrible memories of our sexual abuse.

Beautiful soul, as I look into your eyes through the words of this page, I grab you by the shoulders and let you know that you are NOT ALONE! I was a victim too! Not once but multiple times over a thirty year period. You are not alone in your torment! I have been tormented too! You are not alone in your pain! I have experienced this pain too! You are not alone in your questions, cloudiness, dismay, anger, fear, etc. I have experienced this too.

I have been selected, preyed upon, lusted after, overpowered and drugged. My innocence was taken away also. I want you to feel a sense of relief that you are not alone in this experience. Breathe deeply, a sigh of relief that you have someone that you can speak to you. There is someone who understands exactly what you've been through and understands the deep lows, the confusion, the sense of loss, and unending pain that you have experienced!

Reflection

I laid in the bed facing the wall, four months pregnant, utterly exhausted. My days were difficult, consisting of school during the day, walking to the home of a family friend (since they lived closer), then attending night school. My mother was staying there. She was renting a room because we had been evicted from our home during the summer.

So how did I become a teenage mother? There are a number of reasons that could have contributed to my teen pregnancy. It could have been caused by my father's absence in the home; seeing my mother physically and verbally abused during my childhood; being a black sheep in the family and having a desire to fit in or belong or being a wallflower/late bloomer. Another reason could have been because I was sexually abused ten different times by eight different males and one inappropriate offer. Four of them were family members, one was a close family friend and two were guys that I was dating or talking to.

Four years prior to my pregnancy, on a brisk summer morning, our house was raided by the DEA. My father was what they thought to be a kingpin in South Jersey, though they weren't even close. They busted down our door, pointing guns and commanded everyone to get down on the floor. Women and children were the only ones home while my father was at his other residence, a speakeasy, (a place where liquor and food is sold illegally) in Bristol, Pennsylvania. He was ultimately arrested and charged with a drug felony. Our sole source of income was suddenly gone. He was sentenced to six years in prison, and our lives had drastically changed. We lost everything.

My mother, who was a stay at home mother, went back to work making minimum wage, and my two older sisters started working to assist with the household bills. Our house had eventually foreclosed and we all had to find residence elsewhere. I went to live with my father's family for a short period of time. My oldest sister and her boyfriend moved into a one bedroom apartment in Edgewater Township, and I moved in with her later on. My middle sister moved in with my father's friend's family in Trenton. My mother and younger brother moved into the house in which I am speaking of with a family friend.

Since I had to attend night school to make up for my absence the year before, I came here regularly after school. I would rest for a couple of hours, then walk to the other high school, John F. Kennedy High, which was about 1.5 miles away, to attend night classes. One particular afternoon, I lay in the bed and stared at the wall and wondered, *how did I get here?* I was four months pregnant at seventeen years old, by a guy who I wasn't in love or even in a relationship with.

I decided to sleep with him, because I didn't hold great value to myself anymore and I wanted to be like my peers. The first lie I told myself and everyone else. I had two friends that were very promiscuous and two friends that already had children before we were seventeen, so it sounded right.

Prologue

I was born in Brooklyn, New York on October, 27th 1977. My mother delivered me in Saint Mary's Hospital; I came forth in a breach position and already had a tooth in mouth. My father and sisters just migrated from Jamaica two months before my arrival. My mother immigrated several years prior to prepare for them to join her. Upon my father's arrival he was able to secure a good job as an electrician, which caused us to move within months after my birth to Florence, New Jersey before settling in Willingboro, New Jersey two years thereafter.

My childhood was pretty good as far as I can remember; we had a nice house, vibrant green grass, two loving, yet crazy Jamaican parents and a loving extended family. My parents were very social, because there was always something to celebrate.

Shortly after we settled into our new house in Willingboro, my father was laid off and started dealing drugs. I didn't realize it when I was young, I thought he just had businesses and used his second house to sell alcohol and food to his local friends since my mother wasn't having it at her house.

So how did I get here? Four months pregnant? I continued to ponder what led me to sleeping with a guy that I wasn't in a relationship with. I didn't want to keep his interest nor did I want him to fall in love with me. We were being evicted from our house the next day and I was moving to Englewood, New Jersey (a suburb in North Jersey).

So what prompted me to do this? This would be my second time having consensual sex with a guy. So I journeyed through my mind of my sexual history. My first sexual experience happened when I was seven. I believe this started my fear of being with a man sexually. Although, I wouldn't remember being molested until nine years later.

I found comfort in those of the same sex among my elementary school friends and peers. I didn't know why at the time, but a lot of girls were doing it and I just went with the flow. Around the age of twelve, shortly after my father was sent to prison, my God sister and I were humping with our clothes on in the family room and her mother walked in. We both jumped up and tried to explain away what she saw. I blamed it on my father being absent, and being influenced by some lesbian drug addicts that lived on our block. I knew why I was doing it and knew it was wrong. I told my mother that I would never do it again.

Around the age of thirteen, my sexual friends turned their interest to boys, *Uggh*. I remember a friend and I attended a party one evening and she was really into this boy our age. I danced with boys too, but never wanted anything beyond that. After spending the night over at her house and attempting to "play house," she rejected me. I was sad. The inevitable was happening. All of the girls were moving on to boys and I was not going to go that route. I was too scared. Although I was always attracted to boys, I flirted; fake dated, and had crushes. Sexually I wanted nothing to do with them and I never knew why.

I had my first kiss at the age of ten with my best friend's pseudo cousin. They forced me to kiss him; he was my boyfriend, and I was so scared. We walked all the way down the street with the kids from the block taunting me, saying I was corny, a little girl, a lunch box (yeah that was a name we used). So I did it, while standing on the side of another friend's house. I stood straight with my hands to the side and closed my eyes, frozen like petrified wood. He leaned in and kissed me and tried to put his tongue in my mouth. *Ugh.* It was awful, my mouth was tight, but it was official we were a bonafide couple at the age of ten. They clowned me for being stiff, but I barked back and yelled that I did it. I went through and kissed the boy!

My second kiss would be more memorable as I was starting to open up to experience more with boys. I was thirteen, and went to a house party. One of the attendees was an older classmate, Brian Williams. I would never forget him; I had a huge crush on him, every girl did. He was tall and dark with a thin build. Since I was amazing on the dance floor, I walked past him in the party and he grabbed me, we danced for the rest of the night.

During one of the songs, he turned me around to face him and laid it on me, tongue and all. I was stunned and couldn't believe it for the simple fact that: One, he noticed me, two, he was dancing with me for a while, and three, he kissed me! I was in ecstasy, dazed, but the party was over and he had asked for my number. *OMG "Brian Williams" asked for my number*, I thought, but I had to leave because my ride was heading out. He spoke to an associate of mine and told her to give me his number and to get mine. But she liked him too so she didn't give me the number. *Oh well*, I thought, *if it was meant to be, it would be.*

For a minute I felt amazing, I didn't want to wash my face. "Brian Williams" kissed me, thee "Brian Williams"; maybe guys weren't so bad after all. I ended up running into him one day after school and he still wanted my number and wanted to go steady. *Go steady? What?* My fear got the best of me. I blew him off and avoided him for the rest of the year.

Fourteen was an interesting year. I dated a lot of guys, kissed some too, but I always made up excuses as to why I couldn't go to their house and vice versa. I always met them in a public place while we were with friends. I liked the boys a lot but kept it strictly PG, or he would get his pleasure when we danced close at a party.

During this time, we partied a lot for some teenagers. After one party, my best friend and I spent the night at a classmate's house. It was about six to eight of us laying on a full size bed. I was on the end, a boy named "Nathan" was next to me, and my friend was lying next to him. While they were smooching, I tried to ignore them and fall asleep. Then "Nathan" turned to me and started caressing my buttocks and thighs, *Oh No!* I said in my head. *Please Stop*, I screamed louder in my head. My body tensed up because I didn't want it to happen. I believe he felt my body tense up because he asked me if I was okay. I said yeah, and then he asked if I liked him touching me. I replied no. My best friend told him that I wasn't like that. So that was my sexual experience until everything hit the fan.

So what happened after fourteen? How did I get

pregnant at sixteen and have my daughter at seventeen? Throughout this book, I will go into more details of the different types of sexual abuse that I endured by multiple guys, over a thirty year timeframe, and how it affected my life in ways I never thought. I will explain how I became "Damaged Goods" and what led me to overcome my past, the deep pain and altered mental state to God's Restored Treasure.

Allow me to share some of my sexual abuse experiences.

Prayer

I pray that the words of my testimony and struggle with my traumatic sexual experiences will help you with overcoming your past and pain. That you will gain understanding through my eyes, receive strength and become fully restored from the brokenness that the sexual abuse has caused. I pray that you become victorious and thoroughly healed to live the kind of life that God intended for you.

In Jesus' name,

Amen!

Chapter 1

Molestation

It happened in the winter of 1985, I was seven years old at the time. A family member "Harold" was staying with us because he was having behavioral problems and our family opted to help my aunt. At first he was staying with an uncle in Brooklyn, NY and then my mother's family thought it would be a great idea to get him out of the city and into a suburban atmosphere.

One afternoon, I was playing tag with my two teenage sisters. I would slap them and run away to a hiding spot until they found me and I would have to chase them, hit them again and then run for my life. After about thirty minutes into the game, I slapped them as they were sitting in the room that I shared with my middle sister. I ran into our oldest sister's room and the shut the door behind me, anticipating them busting through the door to slap me back. As I was catching my breath in between laughs, I anxiously waited for the big push. I looked up and to my left I noticed my cousin was sitting in the corner on the dingy orange couch, right next to my sister's closet. He was occupying the room during his stay.

The room was dimly lit because my oldest sister always kept her blinds down and closed, so light barely entered through the pea green blinds. The room had a musky smell of old newspapers since she kept a huge collection of the Sunday funnies, which she read over the years, stuffed in her bottom drawer. I placed my finger over my mouth and asked him to be quiet so my sisters wouldn't know I was in there. He shook his head and continued to read his comic book.

I continued to stand by the door, giggling and anticipating my sisters' arrival, when my cousin motioned for me to come over and sit down on the couch. I whispered, "Okay," as I kept looking back at the door expecting it to open with excitement. I sat down beside my cousin and leaned forward eagerly looking at the door. He motioned for me to sit back and relax; I giggled and tried to explain the game to him. He just looked at me with blank eyes and a slight smile.

He was sixteen at the time, slightly older than my oldest sister. I leaned back and relaxed a little with my eyes still fixated on the door. One of his hands rested behind me on the top of the couch and the other one was in his lap under the comic book. He was holding something but I couldn't tell what it was because the room was very dim. He took the hand that was behind my back, pushed me forward and told me to lick it, that it was candy. I leaned forward slowly toward his hand, opened up my mouth and stretched out my tongue; it was warm and salty. I didn't like the taste, but he instructed me to keep licking it. It seemed like it went on for a while and each time, I would look up to him to see if I could stop.

I didn't like this candy and it didn't taste good. After several times of me leaning over, I sat back and looked at him and asked if I could stop now. He shook his head yes and told me to close the door behind me. I slowly walked to the door, opened it and then closed it as he requested. As I walked out of the room and closed the door, I closed my memory to what happened and avoided him at all costs. I hated his smile and didn't know why. It would be nine years later that I would remember what happened during a series of nightmares and weird daydreams.

I would dream about performing oral sex on a man and visualizing penises in my mouth and not being able to spit them out. These thoughts and daydreams would occur constantly. One day it all came back to me as I walked past my sister's room and I realized that it wasn't a nightmare. This was my confirmation as to why I feared men and older men. I had a reason why I didn't like getting close to boys and I felt more comfortable around females.

Another occurrence happened when I was about fourteen years old; I had spent the night over at one of my best friend's house. We were laying in the family room watching TV and I fell asleep. I was lying on my side with my knees pointing towards the front of the couch. I felt hands creeping up my thighs, and up in between my legs. I tried to squirm so that the person would realize I was waking up in hopes that they would stop touching me. Peering from underneath the cover, I noticed it was my best friend's older brother "Bernard", lying right beneath me. *Oh no*, I thought, *this can't be happening.*

I clenched my legs together to make it difficult for him to get to my vagina, but he persisted. I grimaced as he pushed his fingers back and forth inside of me. It was awful, I didn't want to make a loud noise to alarm anyone, or get him trouble since everyone was still sleeping, but I wanted it to end so badly. I squirmed some more and pretended that I awoke out of my sleep to get him to stop. He finally pulled his hand back and pretended like he just woke up too.

I turned over and thought maybe he would stop since I woke up. After turning my legs facing toward back of the couch, I fell back to sleep. Low and behold, his hands found their way back up my thighs and crept in my underwear. *UGGGGHHH*. I squirmed and groaned acting like I was restless, but he kept on. I swatted my hand out of annoyance and then someone else finally woke up! *Yeah!* He stopped.

I then got up, went into my friend's room, wrapped in a blanket and laid down on her bed. The next day after I went home, I told her what her brother did. She was mortified and apologized to me for what had happened. Shortly after that incident I went over to her house again because we were supposed to go out to a party. Lying on her bed waiting for her parents to fall asleep so we could sneak out, her older brother came into the room. He was telling me how sexy I was, and I instantly became frozen in fear. I lost my ability to move or speak; I just knew that I didn't want to be touched again.

He proceeded to place his hand under the cover and touched me, I lie there frozen, wanting it to end but I couldn't open my mouth. He suddenly stopped and left the room before my friend came back. When she did return, I had to tell her that it was happening again. She was stunned and apologized to me, while we are both lying on her bed. It didn't stop there because he reentered the room and laid on the floor, beneath the bed and proceeded to touch me again. My friend became my voice and informed "Bernard" that I didn't like him touching me and to please stop. For some reason, he felt the need to confirm, and asked me if I liked it. I shook my head no. Then he asked me if I wanted him to stop and I said yes. He then removed his hand out of my panties and left the room. I was still in shock; I just laid there and thanked my friend!

Chapter 2

Rape

When I was fifteen, I was dating a guy named "James" and had fallen in love, so I thought. I just knew if I was going to have sex with a guy it would be with him. We cared about each other a lot and were going steady. Love was in the air.

During the summer I went on a trip with my best friend to New York to visit her grandmother and spend the week with her. For some reason I just didn't get along with her grandmother, she always thought it was cool to belittle me and make me feel small. Even though, I was young and always taught to respect my elders, this mature woman would go out of her way to devalue me, therefore when given the opportunity to correct her when she was wrong, I was happy to do so. I only lasted one day, before we got into an argument and I was calling up my cousin "Darryl" to see if I could stay over at his house.

Since I already had a suitcase full of clothes, I just wanted to continue to enjoy my vacation. Not to mention, my mother was still picking up the pieces of our life after my father had went to prison. "Darryl" wasn't someone I grew up with, nor did he attend many family functions. We became acquainted with each other earlier that year at a party, and had an affinity towards each other. We were close in age and decided we would stay in contact. The last time we saw each other, we were around three or four years old. He made me play house with him and appointed me his wife.

During those years it was completely innocent, I guess. I had to admit, when we met up again for the second time, I noticed that we were attracted to each other. We would dance together at the party until my mother had to come over and tell us that we were actually related, which made it weird but we decided to become friends anyway. After the revelation of us being so closely related, I knew there was no way we could ever be together and we joked about it. I guess in the back of his mind he thought differently.

Shortly after I arrived at his house and settled in, he professed his love for me. I laughed it off because I thought he was joking and I told him that he couldn't be serious; we are first cousins. Our parents were siblings which meant we could never be together. When we were alone, he would grab me and twist my nipple until I gave in and let him touch me or kiss me. After he let me go, I would curse him out, hit him and tell him to never to do that again.

While we were hanging out with his friends or if a guy friend tried to talk to me, he would ask to speak to me in private and make a scene so I would give in and go into his room with him. It was horrible, but I didn't want anyone to know because I feared I would be sent back home early, get in trouble or have his friends and family look at him differently so I just played it off. I still cared about him as a friend and loved him as my family; I just never thought he would take it too far. I figured that he just had a crush on me and didn't know how to handle it.

The first night I actually thought we could sleep in the bed together, but he wouldn't stop touching me and grabbing my nipple. After that, I would never allow myself to be alone with him until he promised me that I could trust him, and he wouldn't touch or force me to kiss him. To avoid being alone with him, I would curse him out or say ok we can go in your room, but leave the door open or you can whisper in my ear.

I slept on his bedroom floor with the door open, from then on so we didn't raise any alarms to his family as to why I didn't want to sleep in his room. I told him if he tried anything I would sleep in his sister's room. Isn't that weird? I cared more about my abuser getting in trouble or being looked down upon then my own safety, but then again I never thought it would go that far. I was willing to accept the physical abuse so that no one thought he was wrong or off. Maybe I held myself accountable for his actions.

It was my fault that he loved me so much. I shouldn't have tried to have a friendship with someone that said they wanted to be with me. I remained on the floor and the abuse stopped, or so I thought. One night, when I was close to going back home, he asked me if I was awake. When I replied yes, he asked me to lie next to him in the bed. When I refused, he made a promise to me that he wouldn't touch me. His fear of the thunder made it so that he couldn't sleep, and just wanted to lie next to me so that he could fall asleep.

I said, "Oh well, you're a dude, deal with it. I'm

not coming in that bed."

He kept whining and wouldn't shut up so I gave in so that we could both get some sleep.

I sternly told him, "If you touch me, I'm back on the floor." He promised that he wouldn't, but within fifteen minutes of me getting in the bed, he started professing his love for me again. At that point, I had it and when I attempted to get out of the bed, he grabbed and pinned me down. I thought to myself, *ok, go through the agony of him touching you for the last time. You will never trust him again.* As I tried to protect my breasts from him grabbing my nipples, he pinned one of my hands under his legs and then grabbed the other one. He aggressively tugged at my nipple again and forced me to kiss him. Then he ordered me to open my legs. My refusal made him grip my nipple even tighter and I began to open my legs slowly. He proceeded to pull down my panties, but I begged him to stop.

"I'll kiss you deeper. You can suck my breasts. I won't fight you anymore, just please don't do this." I pleaded.

Unfortunately that wasn't enough because he advised that he needed to show me how much he loved me. I told him that I believed him and that I knew how much he loved me. I followed up with kissing him deeply. Anything to get his mind off of sex, I cried and begged him to stop putting his hands between my legs.

"Please you don't have to do this, we are related, blood related." I clenched my legs and told him that I would never forgive him. He twisted my nipples tighter and instructed me to relax my legs. I was in so much pain.

The more I begged him to stop the tighter he grabbed my breasts. I reluctantly relaxed my legs, with tears rolling down my eyes. He pulled my panties all the way down to my knees. My tears quickly turned into sobs as he opened my legs wider and proceeded to get in between my legs. The tears continued uncontrollably down my face as he violated my body.

I couldn't believe this was happening to me, he'd move slowly back and forth inside of me while continually professing his love. At that point, my pain had graduated from just physical, to emotional and mental as well. I acknowledged his love for me and pleaded that he stop, but my virtue had gone.

I asked him not to go deep because it hurt and he showed me what deep really was. At times I actually felt pleasure which made me feel even worse. I felt like it was my fault and questioned if I really did want it. I couldn't remember how long it lasted since I had zoned in and out. When I realized that it was finally over, there was blood everywhere.

My knee length nightshirt that I wore was splattered with blood from the waist down; the sheets had blood on it and the mattress was stained. I got up and walked slowly to the bathroom, sobbing some more. I pulled myself together and tried to wash the blood out of my shirt and off of my body in the sink.

I went into his sister's room and she questioned why there was blood on my shirt and I told her that my period came on earlier than I thought and her brother and I had got into a bad argument. I asked for a pad and if I could sleep in her bed with her. When she said yes, I curled up in the bed and quietly sobbed myself to sleep. I was drained and exhausted.

The next morning I woke up and went into "Darryl's" room while he was up and getting ready. He tried to approach me and apologize; he said he couldn't help himself, which was a phrase that I would hear often and would later despise. I lashed out at him and we started to fight. I lost it, I punched and hit him to the point that his brother and sister had to come and break us up. My virginity, the one thing that I held dear to me, had been taken by my own cousin.

I was filled with rage! I hated him! How could he be so selfish? It wasn't fair! Why me God? Why did he have to fall in love with me? Why did you make me so irresistible to the opposite sex? How was I going to tell anyone that I lost my virginity without someone looking at me like I was crazy? It was my fault. I was disgusting. He went upstairs to his mother and I lingered in his room for a while getting myself together.

His brother and sister asked what happened and I just replied, "He's a jerk and always trying to control me." They just felt like we were too close, and needed some space. I went upstairs and his mother was holding his head and kissing his face. My aunt was so upset with me and asked why I had to scratch up her baby's face. Of course I would be the one to blame. But since I hadn't shared what had happened to me with anyone, they wouldn't know to ask what he did to deserve this.

We shouldn't have argued so bad that it got physical, so I apologized to her for hitting him. Now I just seemed like the wild child that everyone had called me to be. I was so angry and I hated him even more, but couldn't tell anyone the real reason why. I just made something up.

About two days after the incident, he rode the subway to Brooklyn with me and we argued the entire time. A family member was going to take me to New Jersey, so I had to meet them at another family member's house in Brooklyn. I cursed him out in front of our other cousins and no one could understand why. We were once inseparable and now I couldn't bear to look at his face.

Chapter 3

Indecent Proposal

In the summer of 94, while my mother was dealing with losing our home, living arrangements were made for me to live in North Jersey with my father's cousin and her family. Even though she was technically my fourth cousin, I referred to her as aunt. It's a Jamaican thing, I guess out of respect since she was much older than me.

When we were evicted from our house, the next day I took the train to Newark, NJ and transferred on the PATH to a stop near his house. I was picked up by another cousin, named "Mike". He was different, like an oreo (black on the outside, white on the inside) but we clicked. I was supposed to stay with them until my mother got stable again. I came to the house and met his older sister, brother and my aunt. It was a great reunion. I started to settle in, made friends with the neighborhood kids, acquired a couple of love interests and partied like a rock star with his sister.

After a couple of weeks of settling in and accepting the fact that this would be my new home for some time, he asked me to come to his room because he wanted to ask me something. My aunt was upstairs but she was very sickly so she wasn't mobile. His older brother was mentally handicapped therefore he wouldn't know what was going on.

We were alone in the house. I sat on the bed and waited to see what he wanted. He showed me his closet, and I clowned him and laughed because he only had white t-shirts and blue jeans. This was back when The Gap only sold those two items. No colors! As I sat on the bed to see what he wanted he asked me to sleep with him and I was puzzled. He asked if I wanted to stay there and of course I said yes. He then repeated himself to which I responded, "No, you are my cousin." I was shocked. *No, not again! Damn what the hell is up with you Dianne*, I thought to myself. *Why are your cousins trying to sleep with you?*

I sat on the bed and thought to myself this cannot be happening. He then got angry with me and told me to get out of his room and that he was going to tell his mother that I had to go. I went and sat in the living room, shocked and saddened.

After he went upstairs and told his mother whatever he did. She called me upstairs and told me that I couldn't stay there. I was told to be on my best behavior and I wasn't. Therefore I had to go. His sister, "Antoinette," came home to see what was going on and I begged her to speak to her mother for me. I didn't do anything wrong, her brother just didn't like me and lied on me. I couldn't tell them what really happened, who would believe me? I went into "Antoinette's" room and lay on the bed and cried. I couldn't believe it.

He kept nagging his mother to contact my parents to get me out of there. He was so nasty to me every day until I left. It was also during this time that I thought I was pregnant from my second consensual sex experience. I went home to only be blamed again for being a problem child, but if they only knew.

Chapter 4

Drugged and Almost Gang Raped

I actually don't remember when this happened but it had to have been between 1996 and 1997. It was February and I was out celebrating my friend's birthday. We went to a club in North Jersey, five of us; the birthday girl, her aunt, two cousins and myself. I wore a red fitted, open back top with straps and fitted black polyester pants.

At the club we did shots of tequila. It was the first time I ever drank tequila. After we partied for a while they decided to go to their friend's house "Jermaine" for weed and to hang out some more. As I walked into "Jermaine's" house, all of the shots of tequila started to hit me hard. I decided to lie down on the couch because my head was spinning. I remember two guys, Jermaine" and his friend "Eddie", taking turns talking to me and my friends also came to check on me to make sure I was okay. One of the guys asked me if I wanted something to drink. I could have sworn I asked for water, but I was in and out of consciousness. Then I remember "Jermaine" started to pick me up.

Even though I was very drowsy, I knew that I didn't want to be moved from the couch so I told him that I was okay. He insisted by picking me up anyway and taking me to a room. He laid me on a bed and proceeded to pull my pants down. I couldn't even sit up without holding on to him, but he just shrugged me off and I fell back on the bed. I could see and hear what was going on in the dimly lit room, but I couldn't really move or speak. I was disgusted and shaking my head in my mind, no.

"Jermaine" then entered my temple and had sex with me. It may have lasted fifteen minutes or so. I started to cry and I was waving my hand like *noooo*, and mouthing no, but no sound came out and my hand barely moved. He then opened the door for the second guy "Eddie" to have his turn with me. As I laid there in horror, for what was about to happen, not only would I be raped once but I would be raped twice by men that I didn't even know.

I tried with all of my might to wave my arms and hands toward them to stop them, but I couldn't move my limbs at all. I tried to scream as loud as I could but no sound came out. I began to cry more and then I could hear my friends calling my name. They busted in the room and stopped the second guy from having sex with me. It was my friend "Shanice" who said, "Oh No, you guys are not about to run a train on my girl!"

I cried so much at what happened and what would have happened if my friends didn't come looking for me. They picked me up, pulled up my pants and carried me out of the apartment. I blacked out and didn't even remember going into their cousin's house to spend the night. They emphatically apologized to me the next morning and I told them that it wasn't their fault. They told me that they didn't know those guys were like that. We tried to piece the night together and identify what they could have slipped in my drink that would make me so numb.

When I woke up, I sat there on the bed and all I could think was *what the heck? Come on God, why me? Why was I a victim again? What did I do to deserve this?*

I was grateful that I was rescued by my friends. But what haunted me was the fact that I don't even know if the first guy, "Jermaine" put a condom on. While my friends were preparing breakfast, I just sat there at the table grimacing at what happened, what more could have happened and the pain that I was in.

Chapter 5

Violated

It was around the summer of 1999, and I was about twenty-one at the time. I had been stripping for about eight months, going to school in Brooklyn at LIU and hanging out with my family. Since I was getting my life together, I became closer to one of my aunts. I hung out around her house more often, so me and another cousin "Derrick" became closer.

We were family and grew up together so there was never any attraction. I looked up to him as my older cousin. I had my own car so I used to lend it to him while I visited my aunt or hung out at their house. I was very affectionate and used to lean on my cousin while we were watching movies. I was happy just to finally be cool enough to hang out with.

While we were growing up, he hung out with my

older sister and other cousins while I was left back with the younger kids. He is a little older than me so I didn't think much about our relationship. When I would spend the night, I would lay in the bed with him and have no worries.

One night I went out to a party and met up with a family friend, who was very close to my cousins. There was a budding attraction for each other for about a year and I'd gotten older so I flirted more often. I went to the party to see him and we took the party upstairs to his apartment. One thing led to another and it got very heated. He was just way more than what I was used to, so I could not finish our hookup that night. I had enough! I went back to my aunt's house and then crashed in my cousin's room. I got in the bed wearing my track shorts and a tee as usual.

I was awakened by his hands on my bottom caressing me and I'm like *Nah. Not him, nahhh.* I thought maybe he was just trying to get a sneak feel while I was sleeping and when I woke up he would stop. Boy was I wrong. It wasn't until I started to squirm that he stopped. *Whew, Ok yippee I'm in the clear.* Then it started again and this time his hands were moving between my thighs, under my shorts and then underwear. I squirmed again and swatted his hand from my bottom. Once again thinking my movement might trigger him to stop.

The third time, he licked his fingers and put them inside of me. I moaned, "Noooo," but that wasn't good enough because he then entered me. My thoughts took over yet again. *What the fuck? Not again!! Nahhhhh, ewww you are my cousin! What the heck?!*

It happened so quickly! I think he did a few strokes before he finally stopped, because I was moaning *no* and pushing him away. I don't know why I didn't fight more, maybe because I just got close again with my family I and didn't want to alarm his mom. I was really shocked that I was a target over and over again. When I got up, neither of us spoke a word about it. A second incident would happen which I would detail in an upcoming chapter.

Chapter 6

Groped

It was after I rededicated my life to Christ. I finally ended a relationship and premarital sex a few years before. I was now sold out to Jesus and I let every guy know that I would not have sex before marriage. I talked about it, but I knew I wasn't going to do anything. Unless, I went back to my ex or after my wedding day with my husband; my ex was the only one that would cause me to lose my control and give in before I got married.

I started talking to this new guy, who was a Christian, but he loved to talk about sex. I would joke with him and told him that although he fantasized about me, he couldn't handle me. It was our running joke.

We started out sexting, and it was good just to talk about it. I would get my relief from talking about sex, instead of actually going through the act. It was our thing. We were friends for a while and he had a crush on me. When we decided to actually talk seriously, I had to admit by that time, I developed a crush on him. He asked me about my sexual history and I didn't hold anything back, I told him about my sexual abuse and he was like ok. One night he came by my house, we sat outside and talked for a while, as he was leaving to go into his car. He grabbed me from behind, started kissing me, unbuckled my denim shorts and placed his hand down them and then inside of me. It took me off guard.

I wasn't expecting this, not from him! He's a Christian!! I told him no, we couldn't have sex, he might have said why? I have a condom. I was like huh? You came expecting to have sex with me?? Through the haze of emotions, I resisted his strong advances. I told him that he had to go. Now I was attracted to him, but I was adamant about not having sex. He used to say that he wouldn't have sex with me before marriage too. Therefore it really puzzled me.

He called me later on that night and apologized for being so aggressive. I accepted his apology and he said, I just couldn't help myself! At first, in my head I was like *yeah most men can't. It's okay.* I related it to my love for food. I was so oblivious, brushing off his actions and lack of self-control, assuming blame because it's just something about me that men just can't resist. We talked occasionally thereafter but it never materialized into anything serious. I actually forgot about it until I started writing this book and listed all of my unwanted experiences. It made me realize this reoccurring phrase from all of these men. *"I'm sorry Dianne, but I couldn't help myself."* This was a phrase that put the onus on me, like there was something about me that defied every man's strength. Was I every guy's kryptonite?? Every man's weakness?? I wasn't even dating him and this was the only time that we were ever alone.

I was a Christian now, this shouldn't be happening to me, right? He's a Christian man who loves God and follows his direction. I thought all of this sexual abuse was behind me. I thought I was healed and delivered from this curse. What did I do wrong this time God? How did I end up in this situation? Will this always happen to me? Can I not trust men? Am I not able to have a relationship that isn't based on sex?

I thought back to when we started talking and he would complement my shape and I told him that although, I appreciate the nice compliment. I had more to offer than my outward appearance. I also apologized if I only displayed my outside appearance as the primary thing I had to offer instead of my other qualities. He told me that I was being too sensitive and his compliments are just that. I needed to relax because it wasn't that serious. I was too uptight.

So here I am being told that I shouldn't respond in a negative way when a guy constantly compliments my shape. I should just accept it because I am appealing to the men. But now it took me back to place where I thought I left years ago. It has me thinking that you are sexy and this still defines you. It's not part of me like I thought it was, it is me.

Chapter 7

Rape while Dating

This nightmare occurred in my thirties. I had been talking to a guy on and off for a while. We previously had sex a couple of times before, and I was very much attracted to him, although I didn't want to have sex this particular time. He had done something wrong and I cut him off for a period of time. So this was our first time seeing each after four weeks of no communication.

I was in the neighborhood, he wanted to see me, so I decided to pay him a visit and hang out with him before he had to go into work. He worked at night so we had about an hour and a half maybe an hour to see each other. We laid on his bed (he didn't have an actual living room, so his bedroom was his living room) and watched my favorite show Scandal, then another show came on.

I went to the bathroom and when I returned, I noticed that he was looking at me like he a lost puppy dog. I leaned in to kiss him, thinking that it would only be a kiss and we would go back to watching TV. As luck would have it though, he sat up abruptly, got a hold of the button on my pants and zipper.

I yelled, "Nope! We are not having sex, you don't deserve it and we don't have enough time." We had 15 minutes before he had to leave for work. I tried to hold my pants up but he flipped me over, held my arms and got my jeans right below my hips, and entered me from the back. I was lying on my stomach in an awkward position, and in so much pain.

While he proceeded to have sex with me, I told him that it really hurt and all he could say was, "that's what you get for making me wait so long!" *Wow! For real?* Words couldn't even describe how upset I was, he finished in ten minutes; he busted his nut and just laughed it off. At first I didn't even realize it was rape. He was someone that I was talking to/dating. They don't consider that rape. Once again, I didn't mind having sex with him. I just didn't want to have sex that particular night and in that particular way.

I punched him and actually wanted to have sex again so I could at least reach my peak. *Shoot! If we were going to do it.* I yelled, cursed and punched him. He laughed at what he did and how I responded. I couldn't get any pleasure. I was his property and I owed him for making him wait so long. I left his place in a huff, and when I got home I was still in a lot of pain. As I replayed the moment, it made me think about when my cousin "Darryl" raped me. I felt dirty and used. It wasn't loving; it was painful and he didn't care.

He actually said, "That's what you get for making me wait so long!"

Like for real? I deserve it for making you wait, like I am obligated to have sex with you and we aren't even in a relationship? I found out he was actually dating someone else, which is the reason I didn't want to have sex with him in the first place. The nerve of him, he was such a jerk. Like really? He was entitled to having sex with me because of?

Later on that night; he texted me and I told him how angry I was at him. It wasn't the fact that I didn't get to reach my peak, but how he handled me. I felt like a piece of meat; he subjected me to pain, and placed me in an awkward position. He apologized and said he didn't mean to treat me like that. He actually really cared about me. But I was so disgusted. I stopped talking to him for again for another week. I never wanted to admit that he actually did rape me.

It's hard to wrap your head around the fact that a guy you are dating can rape you; your boyfriend and husband can rape you. Unless you give them the invitation and say that you want it, they shouldn't take upon themselves and take what they think is owed to them.

After that night he would never pressure me to have sex or initiate it. I had to ask or extend the invitation. Therefore, I figured he was truly sorry for what had occurred. We decided get into an exclusive relationship but there were other issues that caused me to draw back and break it off.

A second incident between him and I would happen a little later. After many ups and downs, he took me out to a restaurant called Arirang Hibachi Steakhouse, he wanted to impress me, and we had a pretty good night. He put in the effort to make me happy, opened all of the doors; made reservations, this was A LOT of effort from him.

I had to admit; I was enjoying his company and didn't want it to end. He didn't want me to leave either and asked if I could stay to watch movies. We watched 2 movies. However I expressed to him on several occasions previously that I didn't want to have sex anymore. I had even told him that night when he started kissing me that I didn't want to have sex and he said ok. It had been nine months since the last time we had sex, I wanted to have a relationship without sex and I needed to rebuild my relationship with God. I just couldn't engage in sexual activity anymore. It was a hard task because the chemistry was very intense between us.

On two prior occasions, I wouldn't take off my pants and left in the middle of the night because it had gotten too intense and almost led to sex. The second time he tried to unbuckle my pants, and I held on for dear life and just left. This time, I had a skirt on, but had shorts in the car. He wanted me to just wear his shirt and I told him that I didn't trust him. I told him that I would hang out for a little while, but absolutely refused to spend the night. He reassured me that he wouldn't try anything, and that he just wanted to lay next to me.

It's been a while and we were both exhausted from the many arguments we had over the past year. He was trying to do everything to show me that he wanted to be in a relationship with me. I trusted him that he would respect my boundaries since we spoke about it multiple times and he said he was ok with not having sex. I put my denim shorts and a tee shirt on and we laid down. As usual we started off kissing and he began to touch me. I held on to my shorts for dear life. Once again, I found myself begging him to stop because I didn't want to have sex and he was ok with that.

He tried to get me to give in and I reminded him that we were not having sex I tried to just lay down next to him so that I could get some sleep, but regardless of my plea, he still asked if he could remove my shorts. He wanted to sneak in the fact that he asked because they were denim, like that had anything to do with it. I rejected him again and as soon as I let go of my shorts, he took them off anyway. He slid my panties to the side and proceeded to enter me. I became so angry with him, yet and still, I blamed myself. I should have just gone home. I hit him so many times on his chest, but that didn't stop him. He continued thrusting in and out of my flower.

I expressed to him that I was in too much pain to continue and that I hated him so much, but he just pulled me on top of him. I ended up reaching my peak a couple of times and he reached his. I climbed down off of him and immediately noticed that I had an extremely sharp pain shooting through my flower; something I never experienced before. I couldn't move, and could barely walk to the bathroom. Or I would have went home immediately, but I couldn't go anywhere, even if I tried to shift my position. Therefore, I ended up sleeping over until daybreak.

The next morning, I had so many mixed feelings about me, him, and what just happened. Yes I was very much attracted to him and I really enjoyed having sex with him. But I really didn't want to have sex anymore until I got married. I still didn't view it as rape; just that he pressured or forced me to have sex and lied to get it by any means necessary. I was an idiot for believing that he wouldn't do what he did.

About a month or two after, we finally stopped talking. I was listening to a sermon and had to come to grips that no means no. I clearly told him that I did not want to have sex over and over. He knew I didn't want to have sex even though I was attracted to him. I don't know what made him force me to have sex with him. It brought me back again to my first rape with my cousin

"Darryl". Maybe, he too like my cousin, thought that he needed to force to me have sex so he could show me just how much he cared about me. He just couldn't understand *why* I didn't want to have sex anymore.

As I wrote this book, I struggled with adding this part, but I had to because I was still forced against my will. Other women probably experienced the same thing, and told themselves that it wasn't sexual abuse. But it was... After that experience he got upset that I was upset. This incident unearthed so many issues that I thought I was healed from and ones that I never knew existed.

One day, after the second incident, he told me that he had a crazy attraction to me and that he couldn't help himself. *Great! I haven't heard this saying in a long time, but I always hate it.*

Chapter 8

Why Me?

Once a victim has been sexually assaulted, they always ask themselves one question. *Why Me?* It's the first question that pops up in your mind, hoping to get relief and clarity of why this incident happened to you. I asked this question over and over again, and I tried to come up with my own answers. *You were the black sheep of the family; therefore you were an easy target. You could be assaulted and no on one would believe you because everything bad that happened was always your fault.* Perhaps you were the loner, used to being rejected by everyone. So they singled you out, gave you the attention you needed, and they figured you wouldn't say anything because you liked the attention. *You were bad and it was God's way of punishing you for being rebellious or you were being taught a lesson.*

These are some of the answers I came up with as to why I was singled out, and why God allowed these horrible things to happen to me. I may have been the black sheep of the family, caused a lot of trouble or spoke my mind too often, but that is never a reason for anyone to violate me the way that they did.

I was just in the wrong place at the wrong time. I was chosen because the opportunity presented itself, and my abuser took advantage of the opportunity. The first incident, I was young, naïve, vulnerable; I was innocent. My predator took advantage of all of that because I was just too young to realize and comprehend that he was mentally ill and had previous issues. He noticed everyone in my household was preoccupied and seized the moment.

The second incident had harsh similarities. Everyone was asleep, and he figured that I was like his sister, promiscuous and would jump at the fact that he was into me. Again, too naïve and young to put two and two together to notice he was interested in me. I wasn't a fast girl despite what people thought. I was extremely shy and corny. I could dance and whine up my waist, because I was Jamaican, but it didn't mean that I was having sex with guys.

I had a cute shape and was easy on the eyes, but I never thought I needed to have sex with a guy to gain his interest. I was also a very friendly person that some men had mistaken as flirtatious. "Bernard's" issue was he had an air of entitlement and thought he could have anything that he wanted. When the opportunity presented itself, I was fast asleep right next to him. Somewhere in his brain, he thought I wanted it. With the rest it's similar to the first and second incidents, the opportunity presented itself and my abusers took advantage of it.

This is a question that you are just going to have

to be okay with the answer. There is no good reason

why this happened to you. Why you were selected? Why

you were violated? Why did they choose you? Why did

they make you do the unthinkable? There are a number

of things that went into the selection of you, I just chalk

it up to fate instead of racking my brain over and over

again on why, why, why! Like I said previously, I was in

the wrong place at the wrong time. I just want to let you

know that it can happen to anyone, nice young girls who

don't give any trouble. Ladies who aren't the black

sheep of the family, ladies who aren't curvy, who can't

dance, who talk, don't talk, etc.

The sexual abuse victim doesn't have a name or a

type, it can happen to anyone and the abuse can come

from someone you would least expect. You are usually

caught off guard because you are not expecting it to

happen. For me, *the why* now has some significance. I

went through these experiences to overcome them and

to coach other women how to recover from it. What happened to me didn't break me, like the devil intended it to. My pain has become my praise. I am a soldier because I have overcome so much in my life and you can too. I pray that God gives you peace with the "Why Me," and that as you read on, you become healed, restored and empowered to help others.

Chapter 9

It's Not Your Fault!

IF I COULD SCREAM FROM THE MOUNTAIN TOPS TO GET AT LEAST ONE MESSAGE TO YOU, IT WOULD BE: PEEL AWAY THOSE LAYERS BEAUTIFUL SOUL. PEEL AWAY THAT GUILT AND SHAME THAT HAS BUILT UP OVER TIME. NO MATTER WHAT ANYONE SAYS TO YOU, I AM TELLING YOU THAT IT'S NOT YOUR FAULT! BELIEVE IT AND RECEIVE IT!

I want you to shatter that ceiling of guilt that has loomed over your head since you were sexually abused. This ceiling has limited you! It was a constant reminder of what happened and your role in it. It has haunted you and stunted your growth. It became a measuring stick of who you are and how high you were going to go. It dictated your very growth.

I believe this is a very important point to make,

realize and accept. Every sexually abused victim internalizes this pain and accuses themselves of what happened to them because your abuser places the blame on us! We bear this heavy burden OF GUILT. This is very important to engrain in your head and heart, what happened to you was not your fault!!! I don't care how loose you have been, how you invited the guy to come over, how much you flirted, what kind of clothes you wore, that you liked or loved your abuser at one point, how bad you were, how hot you were, how strong you were, etc. Repeat after me and say it out loud, *IT'S NOT MY FAULT*!!

What happened to you was not your fault! I used to replay the events over and over. I would often think what would have happened if I didn't laugh so much, or if I didn't have a big heart, if I didn't trust him, if I didn't sleep over at my friend's house, if I wasn't a black sheep, and the list goes on. I would try to figure out how I allowed this sexual abuse to happen and how I could avoid it from ever happening again.

I blamed myself for being naïve and trusting my cousin "Harold" at the age of seven. When I remember what happened to me. I was disgusted at myself. I thought, *you should have known that wasn't candy; you should have sensed he was creepy; you should have ran back out of the room when your sisters didn't come looking for you. You shouldn't have made eye contact with him!*

I blamed myself for staying in that room. I assumed the blame for years and carried the guilt of what happened. But it wasn't my fault! I was seven years old! I finally realized that there was something called consent, and no matter what, it had to be given. I was happy because I was playing a game with my sisters. I sat down on the couch because I was tired from running and laughing. I sat next to "Harold". No one said he had mental and behavioral issues that I should stay away from him. I didn't know what else there could possibly be to lick other than candy. I was young and I believed a guy that my family thought was okay to be around me. It wasn't my fault!

With my best friend's brother "Bernard", I didn't know he was interested in me. I didn't think it was unsafe for me to fall asleep around him. Nobody warned me, he never gave any signs that he would be a threat to me. If my family trusted him, then why wouldn't I? It wasn't my fault!

With my first rape, I never would have imagined that he would rape me or even try to have sex. Kissing cousins is one thing, but sex and rape were an entirely different entity.

Then there was my second cousin "Derrick". How could he be attracted to me, especially to the point of having sex with me against my will and while I slept? I would have never ever imagined that one. I was totally blindsided. It wasn't my fault! Your abuser may say, *Why did you come over? You knew what was going to happen. Why did you kiss me? Why did you get aroused?*

Sometimes our abuser puts it into our heads that it is our fault. We asked for it, we wanted it. But they are wrong, it is their fault for not asking for your permission. It's their fault for lying about what they were asking you to do, especially if you were a child and molested. It's their fault for thinking that they deserve to violate you. Stop blaming yourself for their actions!

Most likely your abuser thought about violating you long before they actually did. Probably the first time they came in contact with you. It's called grooming, they groom their victim, buy their trust and then lure them to a place or position where they can abuse you. You are most likely unaware of it until the abuse is happening.

Stop blaming yourself for being at the wrong place at the wrong time. Stop blaming yourself for being beautiful, shapely and naïve! Stop blaming yourself for being vulnerable and wanting attention! Stop blaming yourself for trying to act older if you were lying about your age! Stop blaming yourself for having one too many drinks that day/night! Whatever you feel that you have done to contribute to that horrible act! It's NOT YOUR FAULT!!

Even if you were raped by a guy you dated or liked and invited him over, got undressed then changed your mind. You have that right! It's your body, no one has the right to your body except for you and whoever has your permission! Too often your abuser wants to put the blame on you and denounce their accountability! Don't allow your abuser to place his or her guilt onto you. The last guy that raped me, said to me, "that's what you get because you made me wait for so long." *Huh? I deserve to get raped because I made you wait between the time we had sex and during that time you decided to date someone else which caused me to stop talking to you?* How dare he demand my body when I couldn't even get his undivided attention.

Your abuser may say various comments to validate why they did what they did, to make you feel like it was in your control the whole time. It actually it wasn't, they were dictating the game, they wanted to get their pleasure by any means necessary, and you were just a pawn in their game. They used you and it wasn't your fault!!! Give it back to your abuser and set yourself free from the burden of guilt, that you caused this horrible abuse upon yourself.

It could have happened if you weren't trusting, drunk, young, old, vulnerable, etc. Please know that everyone has the right to free will. God hasn't given women the power to control her actions and denied men that ability. We all have the ability to control our actions. It could happen to anyone, you have self-control and the person who abused you did not operate in self-control. When you tell someone NO, that's it right there! I didn't mean yes, go ahead, I didn't say this is okay; I didn't say I want this right now, proceed. I didn't say yes I like this, keep going or do it again! I SAID NO!!!

You probably have said NO multiple times. Your actions indicated NO. Some of you were drugged like I was one time and you were incapable of even saying NO, because you were incapacitated. It's still not your fault! You may have drank too much too fast, tried a new drink you weren't familiar with how your body would react. But you were with friends and thought you were safe, you didn't know your friends had friends that were rapist!!! It's still not your fault! Some of you weren't even old to understand what was going on! You may have even felt gratification during the act! That still doesn't mean it was your fault and that you wanted it!

Your sexual parts may respond to touching in a positive way, but it doesn't mean you asked for it and knew what was going on. They went beyond the limitations and crossed a forbidden line, you didn't put a gun to their head to make them violate and abuse you. They didn't respect your words or you! They knew that what they were doing was wrong and they did it anyway, because they had an heir of entitlement! They are mentally ill! Not you! They needed to be in control to get what they wanted! But whatever their reason was for abusing you, know that it wasn't your fault!

After hearing *I couldn't help myself* for the umpteenth time, I internalized the guilt to hatred, and I began to hate myself. I hated this power that I had over men that made them want me so bad that they felt they had to rape me. I felt for so long that I was to blame! I was too sexy for a man's restraints; they weren't built strong enough to resist me.

It even crossed family lines, into incest; no man could withstand my sexiness! It was horrible living with this guilt. Because I didn't know how to turn it off. I don't care how sexy or enticing you may have been that day, God has given everyone self-control! They had no right to violate you or me!

Even with the last guy who raped me, I blamed myself over and over. I should have gone home when I had the opportunity. I shouldn't have wanted to be around him. I shouldn't have gone into his house. By my actions I was letting him know that I wanted it; I wanted what he wanted despite what I said out of my mouth.

I had to really address myself and say, *no you made it extremely clear that you didn't want to have sex on numerous occasions; you spoke about it and told him why you didn't want to have sex. He KNEW that you didn't want to have SEX!* They all knew! I said NO, very clearly! I often thought about this in terms of property. I have seen some amazing comic strips that break down consent!

There's one in the UK that talked about consenting to sex in terms of tea. It gave it a lighthearted take on how to understand what it meant for a woman to give consent. My own example of consent is similar to that of a car or a house.

If I have a shiny car and I'm proud of my achievement, I want to show off my car everywhere I go. I am not giving someone consent to take my car and drive it when they feel like it. If I want someone to drive my car, I'm going to give them permission. Even if I said someone can drive my car and then I changed my mind for whatever reason I choose, they cannot come and take my car without my permission.

Lastly if I allowed someone to drive my car before, that doesn't give them consent to drive my car every time they want to. I have to give them consent every time to drive my car. We could be sitting in my car, and I'm showing them all of the bells and whistles of my car. That still doesn't give them permission or consent to take my keys and drive it.

You see if someone takes your car in any of these scenarios you would be upset and not assume any of the blame. You would hold that person accountable for their actions. Even if you giggled when they drove away for whatever reason, they still took your car without your permission. Correct?

Let's take a look at another example in the case of a minor. If a minor says okay to food from a stranger or a close family resident, they do it because they don't know any better. They entrusted them since the person offering is older, that they should know better and not offer them something that is bad. It's in a child's nature to trust adults or those older than them, especially when they're under the age of ten.

Another reason that I came to understand, as I was speaking to women and just looking at society.

Women are always told to cover up, dress appropriate, if you don't want to be approached or treated like a whore. This puts the entire onus on the female. The male is not responsible for his actions, you are. This ideology implies that women have control over the man's actions. This has been imbedded in our brains as youth and we believed it, so much so that we blame ourselves when we are sexually abused!

Beautiful Soul,

You are not to blame, even if society says so. If the possessions of others cannot be taken without their permission, therefore neither can yours. Your body is a precious gift that shouldn't be touched or entered without your consent. IT WASN'T YOUR FAULT!!

Prayer

Lord help me to accept that I am not to blame for being sexually abused, no matter what I did. The person that abused me is at fault. They violated my body without consent. Help me to give this burden back to my abuser and finally relieve myself of this guilt that I have been carrying since I was sexually abused. I thank you Lord for the hearing my humble cry.

In Jesus' name,

Amen!

Chapter 10

Tell Somebody!

After I was raped by my cousin "Darryl", I kept my mouth shut and internalized all of the pain and the agony that I experienced. I was embarrassed because I had my virginity taken by my cousin. I didn't want anyone to look down on me. This is something a lot of victims of sexual abuse do. They keep it to themselves and try to forget about what happened to them.

In my case, I had always been a very private person. But I believe I didn't say anything to protect my cousin, to prevent division in the family and ostracism. I didn't want him to be looked down upon and hated by some members of the family, nor did I want my family to have to pick a side. So I kept it to myself. I didn't tell anyone, not friends or any guys that I dated for fear of what they would think of me.

By doing this, I carried this burden for years. I buried it deep in the recesses of my mind and heart. Over time it ate it away at my core, it depleted my self-esteem and self-worth. Thirteen years ago I told my daughter when she was eight. I didn't give her all of the details, but I told her about the first two experiences. I wanted her to be aware of the things that happened to me and to let her she could tell me if anyone touched her inappropriately. It felt good to let it out finally, she cried with me and felt bad that the abuse happened to me. She promised to tell me if anyone came close to touching her.

I didn't want her to go through the pain that I went through, nor the shame that came along with the abuse. I wanted to protect her from the brokenness. She held me tight in her little arms as we lay in the bed together, tears flowed down my face. She told me how much she loved me and how sorry she felt that I had experienced this.

About three years later I told my one of my best friends and we cried together, she hated my cousins for what they did to me. She was shocked that I kept in in for all these years. It felt so good to finally let it out. The more I spoke about it, the lighter the load got. I only told one guy that I dated about my abuse history because I felt I could trust him at the time, and this is when I began to allow God to heal me to be more open about it.

When we share our story with other people, it can do many things. It causes you to acknowledge what happened, your feelings about what happened, and allows you to start to release all of the emotional weight that you felt during and after the abuse. It becomes real and not just a horrible fantasy. It actually happened!

Often times when we hold it in, we prevent justice from being served as well. If you wanted to press charges against your abuser and wait, the DNA evidence can be washed away or removed with time. Even if you don't want to press charges, they can still go on the registered sex offenders list and get help so they won't abuse anyone else. I know it may seem like a hard pill to swallow if your boyfriend or family member abused you and you don't want to cause any trouble. Think about the possibility, though, if they go out there and abuse someone else. How many girls and women could you have prevented from being abused just by sharing what you experienced?

Prayer

Lord give me the strength and courage to tell someone about my sexual abuse. Allow me to find safety in this person where I can freely describe the memory of what happened. Please help them to be non-judgmental, since this experience already made me feel so ashamed. But I know that I will feel another weight lifted off of me and a release in my heart, by sharing it with someone else. When I speak about my sexual abuse, allow me to be liberated from the shame that it made me feel and caused me to keep it a secret for so long. I come to you as humbly as I can.

In Jesus' name,

Amen!

Chapter 11

Damaged Goods

When something is damaged, it is no longer whole. It is usually discarded or casted to the side. It no longer holds the value it once had. Most of the time it is deemed worthless; therefore what do you do with something that has no value? You throw it away, neglect it, or use it for a less than intended purpose. It is not worth the effort, attention or energy. It is of no importance and therefore it no longer has a priority in your life.

Since I am a very visual person when I think of something that is damaged, I think of a store, a grocery store to be exact. If a package is opened before being purchased, the protective seal is broken and the freshness of the product is no longer guaranteed. Nobody wants to buy that item, correct? The store usually "damages it out" (a process in which a store employee takes the item, registers that it's damaged in their system for inventory purposes and discards it or non-perishable goods can be sold to an off price store for lower than its original value).

In cases where the item may not be thrown out, sometimes fruit or vegetation, it may get brown spots. It may be left with the others, but the consumer will overlook this item and not purchase it because they can purchase a perfectly good product which is not rotting for the same price. No one is going to choose the tomato with mold on it because it's not worth the value and it's spoiled. Another case would be a clothing store, if an item has a hole in it, they might mark it down or discard it and once again it also loses its value.

This is how I felt after my cousin "Darryl" raped me and stole my virginity. I actually spoke it and called myself damaged. I was broken, my protective seal was broken, and my goods were spoiled. I was tainted because I slept with my cousin! My first cousin at that! I was like an apple with a huge brown spot, which was rotting away slowly. Who would choose me? Who would pay my original price, knowing that I was damaged? I wouldn't be treated like the other girls that didn't sleep with their cousin; I wouldn't be regarded the same way. Granted I had some issues before the rape, but it wasn't something that couldn't be fixed.

I had been dented by my rebellious behavior; I was experimenting with girls when I was younger which is popular now but it wasn't in the past. I was different, and finally getting myself together; learning how to coexist with people without causing a problem. Then the doozy... not only was I raped, but it was my cousin that raped me. My precious virginity that I held onto so tightly to, and prided myself for keeping through the age of fifteen, was now gone.

All of the other girls my age were giving up the cookies since twelve. My male peers were so proud of me when they found out that my hymen was still intact at tenth grade. Whoop, Whoop! Yeah, I was the crème of the crop, a rare breed and valuable. My male peers praised me and encouraged me to hold out. I was cute, had some style, a Coca-Cola bottle shape and a lot of suitors. I was winning. But that day damaged me, it took my pride. It made me hate myself, my face, my smile, my eyes. I was so broken inside, I lost a part of me that I could never get back. I couldn't fix this, I couldn't be repaired, and I couldn't erase the permanent stain.

After I was raped at the age of fifteen and returned home to New Jersey, I remember crying and sobbing on my bed. I asked God why and wrote in my journal that I was damaged. I sat there by myself and reasoned that I could never get over this, what decent guy would want me? The dreams to fall deeper in love with my boyfriend at the time were destroyed. Why would he want me? I felt so dirty! How could I tell him, what would he say, who would he tell?

So many negative thoughts went through my head that day! Therefore, I created an argument with my boyfriend "James" at the time and told him that I couldn't be with him anymore. He thought it was about a rumor that he had raped some girl at school. How ironic. But I didn't want him to find out and reject me, so I ended it.

Although your experience(s) may have been different from mine, I can imagine just how you feel. I had a gaping hole inside of me that was rotting away at my core, my self-esteem and self -worth. It's like you have an infection that is slowly spreading through your body and starts to deteriorate. Or it's a scar that serves as a constant reminder of when you were victimized. You try to wash it out or cover it up, but it's still there.

You notice it the most when you are by yourself. This damage now dictates who you are; how you act or react to situations and your decisions. You're vulnerable, but you don't want to be. It has weakened you. You feel as though everyone can see the damage and you are extra sensitive. You hold your head down when you walk out in public. You can't make direct eye contact, and when you do try, you do what you can to hide what you know. You assume that you are not good enough or only pretend that you are, but subconsciously you know that you are damaged.

The thought of my rape at fifteen seemed much too bear, then a year later the molestation from when I was seven came back to my remembrance. It haunted me and I fell even deeper into my brokenness. *Great now I was a giving head at seven, you are a sure winner D!* I was so disgusted with myself and what I had done I didn't see any light at the end of the tunnel. I was worthless in my own eyes.

Each incident broke me down more and more. By the time my cousin "Derrick" raped me, it was the final stamp of damage. Any dignity I had, vanished. I was so completely broken, that this was the first time I noticed that I was bi-polar. I tried to overcompensate with schooling to prove that I could be successful to everyone, especially myself. The blame that I carried and the fact that it happened with another cousin; I needed something tangible to overshadow it. I worked harder, but I also battled these negative thoughts. I became very grandiose in my thinking and actions. I tried to finish school earlier than expected, I gave myself false hope of wanting to graduate sooner, but now that I look back, I was trying to prove to myself that I was worthy.

Since I missed my goal, I fell into a deep depression for one to two days at a time. I got more comfortable in stripping and started drinking more during work to get through my shifts. As each incident happened, it just confirmed how worthless I was. Especially hearing the same excuse, "I couldn't help myself," those words seared my heart every time, and it cut deeper and deeper as the guy spoke it out of his mouth.

After "Derrick" had his way with me, I never believed that I would ever get married or have a long stable relationship. I was so broken that I couldn't imagine being around a guy longer than a year. If anyone made it that long with me, he was a real trooper. When the Christian guy rushed me and groped me, I was like *what the hell, no one is immune from my powers?* It was my scarlet letter and I accepted it.

You see the damage is so great that it starts to infiltrate and dictate who you will be. You are no longer you, but a fragment of who you used to be.

Chapter 12

There's Hope!

At this moment, you are probably realizing how damaged you are. You are finally acknowledging those deep emotional issues of feeling hopeless, as if there is no way to erase that ugly stain. In your mind, you've probably questioned whether you'd ever recover from this horrible incident and I can imagine how low you may feel! The sexual abuse has broken you and bringing it back up after all of this time has brought back a rush of emotions; the fear, shame, pain and agony you experienced when it happened. But be encouraged beautiful soul, there is hope!

In 2002, I went to my niece's christening and heard a powerful word about redemption. To be honest I don't even remember what the pastor was saying. I wasn't even thinking about Jesus. I just went to support my sister, christen my niece and go back to the house to eat and party. Remember, I was so damaged that I accepted it; it became my norm. I wasn't seeking any help because I didn't think there was any help for me at that point. I was numb toward my pain, and buried the memories so far down in my mind that I didn't even remember that I was sexually abused. I made it disappear so that I could live this dysfunctional life. But the words that came from the Pastor's mouth spoke directly to my pain and my broken heart.

I couldn't hold back the tears as they flowed out of my eyes down my face. I was in need of healing but didn't know how or who to ask for it. In need of unconditional love, I needed someone that I could release everything to, but there was no one in sight. My heart had been screaming, "Help Me," but there was no one to answer. Until this day, I learned that there was hope for me, even though I didn't fully understand what that hope meant for my situation, I knew that I was tired of lugging this burden around. I rededicated my life to Christ that day. I didn't care what anyone was saying or what they thought. I needed that love so desperately. I had been walking around for years with no hope. No different prognosis of my condition. I was damaged, beyond repair.

But that day, I heard a message of hope. It singled me out in the crowd. It came directly to me and started to break away my disbelief that I couldn't be cleansed, repaired and redeemed. That what had been pronounced over me was not final! Hallelujah!

Because of the amazing grace of God, we have the ability to hope against hope. We understand that even though we have done deplorable things and deplorable things have been done to us, there's still hope! In the word of in 1 John -*If we confess our sins, he is faithful and just to forgive us, our sins, and to cleanse us from all unrighteousness.* In Isaiah 1:18 it states *Come now, and let us reason together, said the LORD: though your sins be as scarlet, they shall be as white as snow; though they be red like crimson, they shall be as wool.* God is sooo amazing that He cleanses us from all unrighteousness, and makes us brand new in Him.

When we receive Jesus Christ as our Lord and Savior, we are made new. Everything that has been done before receiving Christ is completely washed away and we now have a clean slate.

Beautiful soul, you now have hope in which you didn't have before! You thought that the sexual abuse that happened to you couldn't be removed. The memory, the scar, the stain, the pain and the agony was irremovable. But God states in Isaiah for you to come to Him and reason with Him, let's reprove and correct this fault. It goes on to say though that your sins are dark as scarlet I will make them as white as snow. Now scarlet is a very deep red color and the bible contrasts that deep

dark stain with making it white as snow, removing the

color in its entirety. Then it gives us another deep dark

color of crimson, a dark reddish purple, that He will

cleanse and make it as white as wool, natural wool. James

covers everything, your sin and unrighteousness, He will

cleanse you!

Beautiful Soul, you now have hope to know that

God can help you with your damage. Yes you, whatever

damage you have incurred from your abuse, it is not

beyond the reach of God. It is not beyond his limits. You

have hope. I don't care how long ago or recent your

sexual abuse occurred. If your body responded in an

enjoyable way, even if you allowed the abuse to continue

happening, there is still hope for you!

You no longer have to be that broken and

bruised person. Along with salvation comes healing,

therefore if you are broken, hurt or stained from your

past, we have hope that God is able to mend our brokenness. He can fix all of our issues! He is able to remove the pain from the abuse. He is able to take away the hurt from the horrible act that was committed against you and make you whole again.

Therefore we do not have to worry about hiding the scar, wound or be afraid of what people might think or say about us, because of the blood of Jesus cleansing power it totally removes the blemish and heals the wound, as if it was never there. We have hope that this situation will not dictate to our future. We are no longer bound by the shame that the situation has caused. We know that there is a way to fix and heal everything so we can move on and live the healthy happy life that He intended us to live. Therefore your life is not over, this is not the end for you.

When I was raped, I thought that was it. Who would even want me after this? Who would look at me the same? I felt so hopeless that I could never move past that situation. I sank into a deep despair and never imagined being able to be free from the stigma of being raped, even worse by my cousin. I still gave up on myself even though I was a Christian, because I didn't understand His word concerning redemption and hope.

I didn't understand that my life was not over. That there was a way to rid and cleanse myself of this horrible blemish. Some of you just need to know that your damage is not final! The state that you are in is not final! The fear that has dictated your life is not final! Beautiful Soul there is hope even for your situation. Yes you!! Point to yourself and say Beautiful Soul there is hope for me! God can fix that very thing. The hardness around my heart, the wall of guilt, shame, fear, agony and resentment I had toward myself actually broke and the word of hope started pouring in.

I was at the last club I worked at as a stripper in

Staten Island, New York at the time and working

freelance as a ER Tech Technician/Medical Technician

(a CNA that can perform phlebotomy, perform EKG's

and other certified procedures) for various healthcare

facilities as my cover (day job). I then started to believe

that there was truly hope for me. I started to loathe

working at the strip club, every shift was more and

more unbearable. I stopped taking off my top. I started

to hate dancing for dollar bills and within a year I would

give it up completely. I didn't understand what was

happening at the time, but I knew there was more for

me. I knew that at that moment, I was worth something.

Although the money was really great, I started to gain

my dignity back and I was willing to work a regular job

making a lot less money. When I left the strip club in

January of 2003, I never looked back. That was the start

of my journey to where I am today.

It wasn't until 2005 that I actually started to

understand God, His word as it applied to my life and my purpose in His master plan. I understood the word about being cleansed from all of my sins and restoring me, but deep down in my heart I was terrified about my secret and still didn't think I was worthy of God's blessings. In 2006 I was able to share it with a guy I was talking to. I literally told him everything and he was okay with it. It surprised me how easy it was to share my past; I didn't feel intimidated or ashamed. I felt like it was something that happened and God really healed me from it.

Little did I know there was still something that I held onto subconsciously? Although I knew God could deliver me from my past, I didn't quite understand it. I didn't understand His grace as it related to my past. The deliverance piece wasn't clear. I didn't understand how deep my pain was, how it altered my behavior and how God could completely forgive me and cleanse me from the sexual abuse. I didn't realize that I was operating under a mask all of this time. And I still felt that I had to work for God's grace.

As you read on, you will see when I actually allow myself to be vulnerable with God and come to grips with my past and its affects. I understood if I follow him from here on out that I could receive total liberty. Once I was healed and delivered, I was made whole. That my past was washed away with the blood of Jesus and I was brand new. I still couldn't grasp the concept of being born again! I still held myself accountable for what had happened, still blamed myself for allowing myself to be in those situations. I thought like how mankind thinks, yes I was forgiven and set free, but it wasn't forgotten.

Although I kept hearing about how God would bless me abundantly, I still had in the back of my mind a low self-worth. I didn't deserve the blessing because of my past brokenness. I didn't deserve to be happy. I wondered God, how can you forget about all of my mistakes, I did them. But that is the beauty of God, He is not like man. Salvation is a gift that we don't deserve; we didn't earn it and we can never be good enough to do so.

In Ephesians 2:9 it says not by works that men should boast, but by the gift of God. It's a gift. God loved you so much that He has given you this gift of Salvation for free, to be free from sin, brokenness, pain, and you're past! He knows what you have done and what's been done to you! He knows all of your secrets and still sees you as worthy of His delivering power! Therefore knowing this, I was able to hope again that this permanent stain could be erased, this deep grief in my heart could be healed and filled with His joy, and that this brokenness in my mind and body could be repaired. I was not lost cause. I wasn't sick unto death, but there was a cure.

I can imagine that most of you have felt the same way I was feeling, hopeless. That you were bound to this cave and would never be set free, no one could fix you even if they tried, because you were damaged beyond repair. I want to walk you through the amazing benefits of the gift of Salvation. Many people become Christians like myself but don't fully understand all of the benefits of salvation and how they pertain to specific healing.

According to Luke 4. Jesus said that *The Spirit of the Lord is on me to preach the gospel to the poor; he hath sent me to heal the brokenhearted, to preach deliverance to the captives and recovering of sight to blind, to set at liberty them that are bruised.* So you might say to yourselves, so what does this mean to me, I was sexually abused? I'm so glad that you asked. Let's break this down by different types of ailments in the scripture. The first part says Jesus has been sent to preach, speak the gospel (good news) to the poor. You might think well my bank account is pretty full. But this actually means the poor in spirit, your morale is low, self-worth, you think poorly of yourself.

The Greek meaning word for "the poor" ptochos, means to cower down or hide in fear, often involving the idea of roving about in wretchedness. The poor people were always looked down upon and didn't have dignity or pride to stand boldly to beg for money or help, but were low in their spirit. Then, Jesus came to speak the good news to them so they would too know that help was there. They no longer had to be embarrassed or ashamed about their state, because Jesus came to assist and help them out of it.

I know I have been here filled with shame because of my sexual abuse and who abused me. My spirit was fear of people finding out about my past and shunning me. Like the poor I was discarded and looked down upon. I was wandering about in my wretchedness, my unfortunate condition. But when Jesus came, He had good news for me that my situation wasn't hopeless and that help was here!

Secondly, we have Jesus being sent to heal the brokenhearted. You have been broken into pieces, your heart has been torn apart where you once trusted, you live in fear, heartache and regret. You are no longer whole, but your being and life has been shattered because of this sexual abuse, some may question their sexuality, some may question their identity. Your heart is the seat of your emotions and now your emotions are out of whack. Jesus has come to heal all of your brokenness, to put you back together again, to stabilize your emotions. He wants to heal the pain and the sickness that has arisen from your brokenness, restore your trust back in mankind. He also wants to heal you from the inside out.

Third of all, Jesus has come to preach deliverance to the captives. Those that have been taken against their own will by their abuser. They have been held captive in a state of guilt and shame, from the abuse and by their abuser because the act loomed over them. They were bound in a dark place.

I was kept in a dark place for a while, even though I was functioning properly. I was able to still function as a normal person where no one could detect something was wrong with me. I could carry out daily activities, and achieve success, but part of me was mentally and emotionally bound. Even though I would be positive, I didn't like myself and didn't allow myself to be in healthy romantic relationships or I overthought and overanalyzed a lot. Deep down inside, I really hated myself and saw myself as damaged.

Mentally I was unable to detach myself from my abuser, to seek help from or release myself from them. I was captive, held against my own will in the memories

of my abuse, the agonizing pain and mental anguish that

haunted me subconsciously, and manifested itself

through negative thinking. Through this scripture Jesus

is telling you that He has you set free, your captor has

been found and you are no longer a slave or indebted to

your abuser and the sexual abuse you endured. The ties

have been cut! You are set free, the doors have been

opened and you can walk out of your cell with no

repercussions. You no longer have to remain in that

dark place.

The fourth benefit of salvation is Jesus is

recovering the sight for the blind. Whereas in your state

of brokenness, your vision and perception of yourself

and the world were altered. You no longer saw things as

you did before your sexual abuse. You were once

positive and optimistic and now you view everything in

a skeptical way. You tend to say that you are a realist,

but you are expecting and perceiving the worse.

You can no longer see yourself as you once were before the abuse because all you see is the damage or the stain from the sexual abuse. You have been blinded and now Jesus wants to open your eyes so that you can see clearly again. He wants to restore your previous ability to see when you were innocent and pure. So your perception will no longer be skewed by darkness.

Lastly, Jesus will set at liberty those that are bruised. Your life sentence of torment from this sexual abuse has been commuted, you have been pardoned. Since some of us tend to blame ourselves for part of the abuse, Jesus is telling you this guilt that you have carried, has been removed. You are no longer to be crushed or held down by this ball and chain that has been your sexual abuse.

Many of us sentenced ourselves to doom when

this happened, we put ourselves in prison, caged and limited our growth beyond this. But through this scripture, Jesus is telling you that the prison doors have been opened and you are free to walk out. You are free to laugh again, love again, and trust again. The blemish has been completely removed and can no longer reattach itself to you. This is the hope that God has promised us, when we accept Jesus Christ as our Lord and Savior.

These are the benefits that are afforded to us that we, sexual abuse survivors, can look forward to. These promises can totally remove all damage from our past without leaving a trace that it was ever there. We have hope that this sexual abuse would not be the end of us! Therefore let's pray this prayer and allow Jesus to come into your heart to be Lord and Savior, to receive the gift of salvation and the benefits we need to be completely healed and restored.

Prayer

Dear Lord, I come to you acknowledging my sin and unrighteousness. I believe that Jesus is your son and he died on the cross for my sin. According to your word, I come to reason with you, though my sins are scarlet, you will make them as white as snow and though they are crimson. You will make them as white as wool. Your word also states if I confess my sins, you are faithful and just to cleanse us from those sins and all unrighteousness. Therefore let the blood of Jesus cleanse me thoroughly from all of my sexual abuse. The memory, the pain, the brokenness, and guilt that I cannot let go of. Make me brand new as you clean my slate. Redeem me back unto you. I give you permission to repair every part of me that was damaged. I believe that you are able to do everything that I ask according to your word.

In Jesus' name,

Amen!

Chapter 13

All Cried Out

Acknowledging the Pain

Sometimes when a traumatic experience happens, you tend to block it out of your memory and pretend it never happened so that you can move forward without thinking about it. I am here to tell you that you should acknowledge it! There's nothing wrong with acknowledging what happened to you! It's one of the first steps that you need to take in your process of healing. You have to acknowledge that the act did happen!

It wasn't a nightmare that you wish you could wake up from. It was you that it happened to you, a person did violate you and what they did was wrong! Acknowledgement of the traumatic experience is so important because in order to resolve an issue you have to acknowledge that there was an issue. If you cannot acknowledge the problem how do you know what needs to be fixed or resolved?

I want you to go to a mirror and look yourself square in the eye and tell yourself what happened to you. Allow yourself to come to grips that it did indeed happen, it wasn't your fault and it wasn't okay. What you went through was wrong. Acknowledge the pain, the hurt, the emptiness, the brokenness, the confusion, and all of the emotions that goes with the traumatic experience. Allow yourself to cry, yell, scream, get angry, etc. However you need to acknowledge it, it's ok, and it's your pain. But acknowledge it! In the subsequent chapters we will discuss your reaction.

When I finally acknowledged it earlier this year, see I told you that I thought I was over it, but I recently ran into my cousin "Derrick" who raped me and I wasn't comfortable at all being alone around him. He came up behind and grabbed my arm and wanted to take a picture with me. I was very leery of it. I wanted to hurry up and take the picture and get back to the crowd. See it was a simple touch, I was okay when I first saw him and greeted him, but the touch was weird and brought back memories. And as I was writing this book, many feelings came back and cut me all over again.

I haven't relived the detailed memories in years. The pain was unreal and I tried to ignore it, I stopped writing and tried to consume my mind with other things. But the more I ignored it, the more it kept coming back. So one day I had to acknowledge it and I called out my pain and hurt, I cursed and cried. But I realized that I still saw myself damaged after all this time and this damage was not only revealed in my romantic relationships, it was revealed in how I viewed myself overall.

I was fearful of launching my clothing line and

ministry because I felt, what if this sexual abuse comes out. What will happen when people find out that this big name entrepreneur was raped by two of her cousins, molested by another one, and allowed another cousin to have sex her with because she didn't care anymore? How would my business survive this scandal, how would my future husband look at me lovingly? How will my family react, will they hate me all over again because it has played out on a much larger platform?

I had to acknowledge all of my fears that were attached to these traumatic experiences. I had to uncover my wounds, peel back the scab and debride the wound. Debridement is a medical term, which is the process of removing dead or infected tissue from a wound to allow it to heal properly. This is a very important part of the healing process for serious wounds. In my case I healed incorrectly, I masked my pain and didn't acknowledge it, which I will describe in the next chapter. When a wound becomes infected it becomes worse. I know this is not going to be an easy thing to do. But it is necessary for your complete healing.

I had to go to the root of the pain, how it made me feel, the disgust I had for myself, the hatred for my abuser, the emptiness, and the weakness that I experienced during the act. I acknowledged all of it and I cried before God, recognizing all that was broken. It was such a relief. Who knew I was carrying all of this weight for so long? Who knew that this deep rooted pain had manifested itself into other areas of my life? It bred so much negativity and low self-worth that I was subconsciously sabotaging my own destiny. I also didn't even realize that I was still concerned about my abusers and their welfare, how will they be perceived.

It took me thirty-one years since my first sexual abuse to finally have a sit down with myself and God about what happened to me. Thirty-one years to sit myself down and face what had been done, every act, how it made me feel, the blame I placed on myself, the lonely, abandoned, hole I lived in ever since. After I have had my heart to heart conversation in the mirror, I was able to release it to God that He could resolve my issues. I was finally able to open that heavy door to that dark place. It was extremely hard because I never revealed this place to anyone. I forgot it even existed. I was so vulnerable and petrified to show it, even with this loving God.

No one ever knew the state my mind and heart were really in. I was seven when I created it. I was young and innocent and my cousin "Harold" stole that from me. The hurt was so great that I blocked it out so much so that I forgot that the molestation even happened. This is a major step in your process of healing from your sexual abuse. This was a major turning point for me; I finally acknowledged the root of my pain and dysfunction. It exposed that tender, once pure heart that was so badly bruised.

As I cried out to God about how I truly felt, and how broken I really was, tears flowed for what seemed like hours. I did it, I finally did it! I acknowledged my pain! Trust me, I know this might be hard, as you see I struggled even revealing it to God. But I did it. I finally acknowledged what I kept hidden for thirty-one years! I was finally honest with myself about how I felt about being sexually abused. It was a release that I've needed for years.

Beautiful Soul,

If you haven't done this already. I pray you do this now. So you can process all of the emotions that you have masked, buried and tried to forget since you were abused. I suggest that you do this alone, because this is something you need to comprehend and work through. You will feel a range of emotions like I did, you may even be fearful like I was. Because you don't know what to expect and don't know if you can even trust God with this hurt and pain. But Beautiful Soul, you can!

Prayer

Lord I ask that you give me the strength to finally acknowledge all of the emotions from my sexual abuse. Help me to look them square in the eye, don't allow me to turn my head or hide my face. Let me be brutally honest with myself about how I felt when I was sexually abused; help me to open that door to that dark room. After I acknowledge my pain, help me to show you my true heart as well. Help me to let it all out, and allow the tears to flow until I am all cried out about it. Thank you Lord for hearing and answering my humble prayer.

In Jesus' name, I pray,

Amen!

Chapter 14

Don't Mask the Pain!

Many sexual abuse victims mask the pain. We think this is the best way to heal from our sexual abuse and return to a normal life. We believe saying that we are okay, we will be okay. Unfortunately, it doesn't work that way. Saying that you are okay, doesn't address the issue. The issue still festers under whatever you put over it. The wound gets worse, not better. It gets deeper and deeper, becomes infected and starts to affect areas other than the initial bruise or cut.

Although masking may feel great and give you instant relief, it doesn't address the memory of what happened and the damage it has caused. It's the last thing you need to continue to do.

Do you struggle with addiction? Are you drowning yourself in drugs, alcohol, food, or sex, to cover up or temporarily forget what happened to you? You are only covering the issue for a moment in time. After your high has worn off, the pain and the memory will come back. It's a vicious cycle that doesn't end until you actually address the problem.

Some women find comfort in drugs and alcohol, but I hated the taste of alcohol and feeling drunk. It's called self-medicating. I would only drink at times when I stripped to get through the shift. I didn't like to do drugs because I saw many addicts growing up and I never wanted to be dependent on any substance that would make me do deplorable acts and susceptible to being sexually abused again. In my mind I always had to be in control. Because the one that is in control, doesn't get hurt. These were some of the ways I masked my pain:

Ignoring the incident altogether

I tried to pretend it never existed. I thought that

if I didn't acknowledge it and told myself I was okay, that I would eventually forget about it and be okay. Unfortunately my mask only hurt myself in the long term. Yes I may have hid it well from everyone, but deep in my subconscious and heart I was a total mess that I couldn't fix. I tried to forget my molestation at age seven, and it came back to me after my first rape, like a flood.

As I stated before it came back with many nightmares and horrible day dreams. I couldn't forget anymore. I even told myself that performing oral sex on a man wasn't cool and it was for whores. Therefore I found a way not to do it.

Over Achieving:

This is when you have to set high goals and achieve them to gain praise and to feel worthy. Most people with good self-esteem don't need praise or validation from other people or achievement to prove that they are somebody. They believe that they are somebody and just do what they believe they can do. I would go above and beyond because I needed that praise to say that I am somebody.

I would set high goals and challenge myself to achieve it, thinking if I could reach these goals, I would prove myself worthy. In my mind I was labeled damaged and therefore worthless and I had to show people that I was a good person. I wasn't worthless. I believe these were my own thoughts that I projected onto other people. I created this battle with everyone that was only in my mind. I was somebody special. I always dreamed of being someone great, like the doctor that cured cancer. An actress, phenomenal singer, I always dreamed of being someone that people valued.

Gluttony:

Some people indulge in liquor or drugs, I always over indulged in food. It was my comfort. It filled my emptiness and hid my pain. If anyone wondered why I ate so much, I would just tell them that I had a love affair with food. It was hard to tell food that this wasn't working out, but food didn't want to see me go. LOL I would make a joke of it. Whether I was happy, sad, mad, or indifferent, I ate.

I would often go on a binge at times, when I ate until I was so full, food was literally in my throat waiting for the other food to digest. It was horrible. I covered that up with purging in different ways, by extreme dieting and exercise for short periods of time. This was a form of bulimia, but I convinced myself that it wasn't because I didn't make myself throw up and use enemas. I was in such denial. One lie led to another.

Sex:

Some people become sex addicts; addicted to the high or still attached to the need to have sex to feed a deep seeded thought that their sole purpose was to give pleasure to the opposite sex or the one that abused them. Their worth lies in their sexual ability. They are nothing outside of sex. For me I had sex often because in the back of my mind, I believed that that was my best asset to men. That's what they wanted, so much so that it went beyond reason. It would turn my own family members to desire me beyond logic. No matter what I would wear, men would call me sexy and lust after me. Some guys told me that I just had that "It" factor.

I was naturally attractive and ignited some fire in men's loins that they just had to have me. I used sex to show myself that I wasn't affected by this abuse, but actually I was. I slept with random guys just because I could choose to, I was empowered. I told myself that it was because I liked sex and liked to have a roster, a group of guys that I could select to have sex with at any time, but I didn't value it. I didn't care. It was my drug. The high off of the endorphins took away the emptiness and gave me a false sense of happiness. The different guys gave me spice and control. I wasn't sleeping around with every guy, just a handful of guys over the years that I would revisit every so often.

Because of my failure to acknowledge the pain or the actual act of abuse, I just made up reasons why I did things the way that I did. I told the lie so much that I started to believe it. I continually made myself unavailable for a real relationship or when a guy actually made it through my steal wall. I would find a way to end it, saying I was too busy, it's just not working out, you're too good for me, etc.

In addition to my sexual abuse history, I didn't want to end up like my mother, in a relationship where a guy cheated and mistreated her and she stayed. I noticed from a young age that that wasn't love and being that I wasn't whole (damaged), what guy would love me like I needed? I didn't want to endure that rejection and mistreatment, so I rejected and discarded myself before any guy could.

There are so many other ways that we can mask

the pain. I just mentioned some ways I masked mine. We try to convince ourselves that we are okay! That we weren't affected, that nothing's wrong with us. We believed that pretending it didn't happen will make it go away. That you can return to normal life and not have this past resurface, but you are wrong. The pain never died and the heartache was never buried if you never addressed it.

It's not in some grave somewhere, but it has dwelt beyond the surface and has manifested itself in ways you cannot imagine. I was a master at masking my pain. I created an alternate reality for myself. My smile was as fake as a theater mask. My happiness was so fake, I became one of the greatest liars I've ever known. I believed my own lies, to the point that when I went to church one day, a preacher called me out and told me that I was so sad. I looked at him like he was crazy. Sad? Me? Noooo, I have no reason to be sad. He had his daughter pray for me and I believed that I cried, but as I stood there, I couldn't understand why. Why am I crying? Why did he say that I was sad?

I thought that preacher was crazy. When this happened I was in my mid- twenties. We could wear our masks so well, it becomes our face that we forget what we really look like. We take on this fake persona and don't remember who and what we were before we assumed this new identity. Take a minute and ask yourself, how have I masked the pain of my sexual abuse? What fake persona have I created to bury my sexual abuse? How far did I go to hide it? Who and where is the real me?

Think about putting on a mask or a costume and you clean the mask, make sure it's taken care of properly, but you never take care of your actual face. You never wash your face, brush your teeth, and tend to your hair. You forget all about you underneath the costume. Can you imagine what will happen to your teeth, hair and face? Well that is exactly what you have done since you created and put on your mask.

Now it's time to see the real you! If you are like me, you have probably lied to yourself so much that you have forgotten that you are still affected by being sexually abused. You have grown comfortable in your fake life and have come to believe your own lie.

Prayer

Lord help me to see the real me. Expose my masks and the ways that I have hid facing my pain. Give me the strength to acknowledge each mask and give me other ways to heal from my pain. I thank you for hearing my prayer.

In Jesus' name,

Amen!

Chapter 15

Your Reaction is Normal!

I have had a myriad of reactions to my abuse: homosexuality, promiscuity, apathy, eating disorders, overachieving, and workaholic. So don't think you are abnormal with your behavior after you've been sexually abused. Please hear me when I say your reaction is normal!! But please don't confuse this with what I said prior about masking the pain. This is a way that women respond as well, but the former response doesn't acknowledge what has happened, and this can lead to greater harm to you.

I have spoken to many women that have been sexually abused and everyone has a different reaction. I have never judged anyone of how they've responded to their traumatic experience of sexual abuse. I just listened to gain understanding of how women respond so I can help them overcome it or identify with other women that might have been sexually abused. It can be life changing and have a long lasting effect. It's how you respond and cope with what has happened to you. Although some reactions can hurt you in the long run, it is still normal, because it's how you process what has been done and react to get to normality.

As I previously mentioned there are many ways that women respond to being sexually abused to move forward in their lives. I will discuss some ways I and other women have responded. Through these examples you may notice how you have responded and how your sexual abuse has altered your behavior and why.

Homosexuality:

As I mentioned before I have responded in multiple ways, after I was molested by my cousin "Harold" at seven. One way is that I turned to girls, I felt more comfortable kissing girls and acting out sexual desires with girls. Although I was attracted to boys as well, I was afraid of them and didn't engage in sexual activity with them until I was in my late teens. It was automatic and I didn't realize why I chose to be with females instead of males. I just thought males were scary but I never knew why. Not to mention, a lot of my peers were engaging in this activity too and it felt normal. This was a safe place for me, no one made me do anything I didn't desire to do and to be honest it was fun, forbidden but fun.

In my teens when my peers started experiencing boys, messing with girls was old and immature. Therefore I didn't continue in homosexual activity because it was no longer comfortable. For other women, they remained because it was comfortable for them. They feared and loathed men so much after being sexually abused it turned them to women altogether. They never had a desire to be with men, because in their eyes men were the enemy. They were not to be trusted. No man could change this perception because of the hurt; the women were so guarded and convinced that all men would rape them.

To avoid that horrible sexual abuse experience, they did not put themselves in that place ever again. One woman I spoke to early in my years of being an evangelist was a lesbian and I asked her what happened that caused her to be attracted only to women. She told me that she was raped repeatedly at a young age by an older male family member. When she got older she told herself that she would never allow herself to be raped again. She thought she was weak for being raped; therefore she decided that she would become the aggressor. She would take on the role of a man and be a safe haven for women. She would take care of them and show them what true love was.

I thought to myself, *WOW! That is very deep.* That

pain was so great, that she never wanted to experience it ever again. Just under the age of ten, she thought that she was weak against a grown man. She had deep seeded trust issues. The ironic part was that she took on the male role in her lesbian relationships. She cut all of her hair off, she dressed and acted like a male. I used to run into her often on the bus and wondered why she liked women and dressed like a man.

Just being inquisitive, I thought she was beautiful; but she tried to cover up all her female traits, because her abuse led her to believe that being a female equaled weakness. Now isn't that an interesting perspective? She assumed the role of a male to prove to herself that she wasn't weak. That was her response. You see we both turned to the opposite sex for different reasons. I just found comfort in females, where is she wanted nothing to do with her abuser at all, she wanted to be in control and give woman someone not to fear.

Mine was only temporary, hers was permanent. It became her lifestyle. I spoke to her for a while, but her fear was so deep and conviction in her beliefs so great. That this was the only way for her to survive and be free from sexual abuse.

I am also reminded about the television movie, Women of Brewster's Place. It was a story about various black women with various lifestyles that lived at a building on Brewster's Place in Brooklyn, New York. Two of the characters were lesbians and they faced criticism from some of their neighbors. One night after fighting with her neighbors, one of the lesbians was walking in an alley and she came across a male neighbor who was reaching out to her for help. She was a little inebriated and was reminded of her sexual abuse. She picked up a brick and repeatedly hit the older, kind neighbor in his head, killing him.

You see? Her fear also turned her away from

men to women, where she felt safe from harm. The act

of the man grabbing at her took her back to a place

where she felt she needed to protect herself. The pain of

her past clouded the reality that was in front of her.

Now she is grown, stronger and can fight back. The

great fear of being harmed and sexually abused was so

great that she continued to hit this male neighbor until

he no longer moved and she was safe.

This was such a powerful visual for me, how the

hurt and pain was so deep that it subconsciously came

back up and she relived the moment. Do you see how

your sexual abuse experience can affect you and can be

the root cause of why you act the way you act?

Promiscuity/Apathy – Teen Pregnancy:

After my cousin "Darryl" raped me, I became

somewhat of the aggressor. I tried to take control of a

guy I slept with instead of having him take it from me

again. I was very flirtatious even though I still held on to a lot of fear in the recesses of my mind. I needed to be in control so I would be comfortable in the situation. I set the rules, the time, date, when and where it was going to down. In my mind I felt as if I was dominating, even though I had no idea of what I was doing. I was so lost when it came to sex. I just laid there and figured the guy knew what to do. I was also so afraid of being raped again, so usually if I was alone with a guy and he asked to have sex I said yes.

I needed to choose who I slept with. I just needed to have a positive sexual experience if at all possible. Control was my driving motive. Stay in control at all times. Like the woman who turned into a lesbian, she needed to be in control to protect herself from being sexually abused. I too craved control. I learned how to use my sexual attraction as power and would use it to my advantage to make a relationship work in my favor.

If I wanted to date a guy I would entice him with my goods, flirt really heavily and tease the heck out of him, to make him succumb to my demands. They were putty in my hands. I remember the first guy that I chose to have consensual sex with. It was about eight months after my rape and I just needed to be freed. I needed another sexual experience to think about. He was a fellow classmate in my Math Class in tenth grade. I was cool with his girlfriend, but I could tell that he was interested in me, so I flirted hard and he flirted back. He wanted me but he had a girlfriend.

We talked a lot in school, I would flirt with him on purpose to exercise my control, and he seemed nice like he wouldn't hurt me. This was my guy, he would be the one I give consent to have sex to. One night we met up at a school dance and he was with me the whole night, he was caught up and forgot that he had a girlfriend in which he ignored to be with me. I loved the attention so much that it was intoxicating.

Shortly after the dance, he broke up with his girlfriend and he was free to date me. At the time, I couldn't go out much because I was stuck at home watching my nephew, my sister's oldest son. So I passed on dates, he thought it was my baby but I told him that I was still a virgin, well technically I was. I couldn't say the truth and I couldn't figure out who I could lie about to say he took my virginity. I played it cool and skirted around the question. We talked about sex a lot and what he would do to have it with me. I just wanted to get it over with. Sure I was scared but I needed to have a safe experience to erase the old memory.

One day it finally happened, I invited him over in the month of February. It was going down, my mother was working late and no one was home. We chatted for a bit, but we both knew what he came over for. We started kissing and then the clothes came off, he put on his condom and he penetrated me. It hurt a bit and surprisingly felt good. I think I held onto him tightly because it was surreal, I was actually having consensual sex and I was enjoying it. I did it! But I still feared that he would find out about my past somehow by being inside of me. We did it again, *sure as many times as you like, please just erase the mark my cousin "Darryl" left when he raped me.*

Before the second round, he asked me why I wasn't bleeding and I said I didn't know, maybe I broke my hymen with a tampon. Side Eye. Then I told him that he was the first guy that I wanted to have sex with. He also asked why it went in so easily. I was like, "I don't know you tell me, I thought it hurt a lot. Was it supposed to hurt more?" I really didn't know if it was supposed to hurt more. He liked my answers so we left it at that and proceeded with round two.

It was cool, I now had a clean sex story that I can

share with people. I wasn't a virgin anymore by choice! I chose who I wanted to give myself to and I felt absolutely amazing about it. We talked every now and again, but I most likely drifted away. During high school I started doing hair for the women and peers in my neighborhood.

My daughter's father was a grandson of my client and I started hanging out at their house. I was cute and sexy; all the guys were interested in me, but I maintained my cool. I became friends with him and flirted with him. He would be become target number two. He and his brothers had girls running in and out of the house, and I really didn't want to be another chick on their hit list so I fell back. He thought he was suave and had game, but little did he know. I really didn't care much about giving up the cookies.

It was the night before our family was to get evicted from our house. I was moving to North Jersey and wanted to party with my local friends and get one last hoorah before I left to a new town. Earlier that week, I told his older brother and friends I was leaving and word got back to him. He tried to flirt with me harder so he could get the cookies, I played coy, as I made my last rounds to my friends' houses. I came back to his and I was told he was waiting for me upstairs and wanted to say a special goodbye. I knew what it meant and I was like, whatever. *He seems like a cool person, I can do this.* So I went upstairs and we talked briefly, climbed in the bed and he asked me if I wanted to give up the cookies.

He was nice about it and I said sure. I was on my back, he got on top. It was less passionate then my second *first* time, but hey whatever. I laid there and let him do him. When he finished, he asked if I wanted to do it again and I said yes, so we did. I woke up a couple hours later, said my goodbyes and walked out the door.

Since I wasn't too keen on sex I didn't know how to make sure a guy put on a condom, I didn't know anything. I really just laid there and allowed him to have sex with me. I didn't care.

I needed another experience to push me past my rape and who knows who I would meet in the new town. So a month later it was August of 1994. I was speaking to my best friend and noticed I had missed my period. We laughed, thinking it would be funny if I got pregnant, not! Out of all people, the girl that didn't sleep around until this year was pregnant. What a great joke. So this was how my life shifted quickly, one bad decision to just sleep with a guy that I wasn't in a relationship with. I didn't love. I just wanted another guy to say I CHOSE HIM and I CHOSE to have sex with him. It was my CHOICE! My terms, nobody took it from me.

So this is how I got here. I was four months

pregnant, going to school twice a day, staring at the wall. My reaction to being sexually abused and molested caused me to be here. Who would have thought I would be here? I was only trying to erase the memory of my abuse and create new memories. I didn't even know how to engage in sex properly, I was winging it. I just wanted to choose who I slept with and who I didn't. I was empty and just needed to fill myself with something. I was numb and needed to bring myself back to life. I needed to entertain myself to pretend that I was ok and normal. I needed to blend back into society, but I had to be in control.

I didn't care about falling in love anymore; it wasn't an option for me. This lasted up unto my mid-twenties, using my womanly wiles to control a man. The outcome of relationships was how I dealt with my pain, filled my emptiness, created a false sense of worth and high self-esteem based on my outward appearance and shapely figure. This lifestyle became my norm, flirt with a guy, talk to him for a short period of time, have sex, after I got tired, break it off with him. *Next! What's up sir, what do you want? Oh you like me huh?* Next target.

I really hated men for a period of time and I really wanted to make them suffer for their weakness of being attracted to me. Although I didn't use men for money, sometimes I had wished I did. I had morals that I could bank on, but I used it to get my way. I couldn't date a guy I wasn't attracted to; I could only fake it for so long. He had to hold my interest some way or somehow.

Despite my apathy, I was able to have two long term relationships. They managed to withstand my abruptness and saw past my hard exterior. They were persistent and loved my façade.

Sexual Entertainer/Stripper:

I became a stripper at the age of twenty-one. I told myself it was to make money to finish my degree and to cover my expenses while I was in my full-time program for a Physician's Assistant. Since men lusted after me anyway, I figured why not make money off of it. I enjoyed the game of creating a fantasy for them and allowing them to be putty in my hands, by twisting my hips and licking my lips. I coupled this with my promiscuity and just slept with guys for the heck of it, because that's what they wanted anyway, right. No love at all, just because I had great sexual attraction, I knew they wanted it and if they were good enough, they would be rewarded with my body.

After the sexual experience I would get up and walk away at any time. I was never fully invested. I always made sure to keep a certain level of disconnect. They knew how much I wanted them to know, and I gave only a part of my heart. I made sure to never fully fall so I always had a way of escape. I needed to be in control.

Along with stripping came drinking and drugs. I started to smoke cigarettes more and then marijuana, beer and alcohol. When I started working in the strip club, I needed to be really tipsy to heighten my sexual prowess and overcome my fear of taking off my clothes in front of strangers. It loosened me up and helped me to blot out some of my moral conscious. They call it liquid nerves. I started out in a small club in Philadelphia, Pennsylvania. I think it was called Diamond Dolls. I went by the name Karamel, eventually I would shorten it to Kara. That was my escape; I developed a strong tolerance to Tequila and Vodka, learned how to master pole dancing and perfected my skill of temptation. I oozed sexiness.

There were many nights that I didn't want to

work the crowd, I just enjoyed the atmosphere, sat down with one of my regulars or a random new guy that came in that fell in love with me on sight. I would keep about four or five guys that I would sleep with and rotate when I got bored. It was good when I had a guy to go to, so that I could release all of my sexual fantasies on him that I created at work.

When I drank, my sexual prowess was heightened and my libido was in full swing. I needed to give him my all and then leave early in the morning, go home, sleep and start all over again. I lived a double life and I loved it. I was Dianne by day and Karamel or Kara by night. I was in control and I was safe. I still kept my day job and used my power of attraction at work to gain favor with the male staff, especially the doctors and therapists.

It felt good to be wanted and have choices, even if they only desired to have sex. I was okay with it because there wasn't much that I had to give. I wasn't the girlfriend type. I didn't want to be locked down by any guy because of fear of rejection if they found out my deep dark secrets, and I didn't think I was good enough to be loved anyway. I was damaged and I couldn't love them properly even if I tried.

I believed that sex was all I had to give and that I wasn't worth much after my cousin "Derrick" raped me. The second time he had sex with me, I just didn't care, I allowed him to enter me without saying a word. It was New Year's Eve, I don't even remember what year. I was laying on my aunt's floor with some cousins and my daughter, I think. While everyone else was fast asleep, I saw him coming in the room. He laid down next to me, pulled my underwear down, entered me, did his thing and then got up.

There was even a time after my Aunt's funeral; I was laying in the bed with a younger male cousin at that time. He was about 3-5 years younger. I think he probably had a crush on me for a while.

He asked me if he could see what it felt like to have sex with me and I agreed! Why not? Here you go, I really did not care. I guess word was going around that I was the family whore. If you needed to bust a nut, go to Dianne. He put his little thing in and did a few strokes, then felt bad I guess since we were cousins. We stopped. I was really gone then. Sex didn't mean much to me anymore.

By 1999 I really just didn't care that much about myself. I believe in 2000 I took a customer home from the strip club, the first time I would ever do this. I would date some of my customers or just talk to them, but I never went home with one right after a shift. (the second one became my boyfriend). We spent at least half of my shift, anywhere between three to four hours, in the champagne room. He was a white guy that fantasized about being with a black girl. Like some do. He wanted me to be his first, sure why not, he was actually cute. He offered me money, but I didn't take it. I wasn't a prostitute. That was one rule that I wouldn't cross. *If you want to sleep with a guy, sleep with him, but not for money.*

I saw many girls do this but I just couldn't. I was so drunk, he drove with me in my car to his place, his friends followed in a separate car. Thinking back, this was very dangerous because this guy could have killed me. I guess my grandmother was praying for me like crazy. The customer and his friends went to the same university as my ex and they thought they knew him. I even called my ex from their house and asked him. He was livid!

This was going to be the first white guy I would sleep with. Thank God there were no camera phones back then. His friends tried to keep the door open, but I made them close it. It was an interesting experience. But like most, we had sex back to back then, fell asleep, I woke up in the morning, put on my clothes and left. I don't think I ever spoken to him again. The apathy that I exhibited was dangerous at times. I was so detached. The second customer I would sleep with became my boyfriend and truly the love of my life. Although it didn't last, it helped me to see myself as capable of being in a lasting relationship and possibly married. He hated the fact that I could just walk away at the drop of a dime.

Mental Disorders:

Bi-Polar Disorder, Anxiety and/or Depression

Many people react to trauma differently. Remember what happened to you? You were traumatized by what happened. Therefore your mind automatically tried to find a way to cope with what had happened. Anxiety is fear, fear of what happened may have haunted you. It definitely haunted me and dominated most of my life, since my first molestation. I lived in a state of fear and panic, it got worse as I got older.

I remember as I child I actually used to be shy, then I became outgoing. I learned that this was a protective measure to hide my vulnerability. If anyone really knew me, they knew I was this big crybaby. I was soft as a pillow, but I would act hard as a rock to cover and protect my soft insides to prevent me from getting hurt. It worked; so many people thought I was this big outgoing person, when I was just trying to mask the fear that dominated my life. Isn't that ironic? I acted like the very thing that terrified me.

My bi-polar was an outward expression of who I was. Two types of Dianne battling every day, I was either hot or cold, loud or silent. I went from one extreme to another depending on how great my fear was. If I was in a non-threatening environment, I was very quiet. The real me came out. If I was in a threatening environment, I was on high alert and felt the need to show that I wasn't afraid. I had to be loud, crazy and totally uncensored. This became my norm and what people perceived me to be. People expected me to be loud, funny, rebellious, wild and crazy, so I was. Trying to cope with the fear that the sexual abuse produced.

My terms, *nobody took it from me*, manifested itself with this dual personality and later depression. The fear of actually being vulnerable, produced high anxiety that became paralyzing fear. In 2014, my daughter actually noticed my bi-polar disorder. I was unable to mask it anymore. I was swinging from one extreme to another so bad. I completely lost the focus I once had, my temperament and my ability to mask my fear.

I was suicidal at times for years ever since 2006. I thought about it often, I couldn't cope with the fear, failing or not being successful. Coming into Christ and losing my masks of sex, drinking and overeating, I began to head into a downward spiral.

In 2016, I became very suicidal, and the anxiety had reached its peak. The thing that I feared the most came upon me. I lost all of my control. I wasn't strong, I became weak and vulnerable. I wasn't as independent as I used to be and I couldn't figure how to get back up. I was so depressed, the remembrance of my sexual abuse was strong as I wrote this book and I couldn't cope like I used to. I had to let go and trust God. Someone other than myself! Me, give power to anyone? Never! But I couldn't ignore my mental issues anymore. I had to face them.

Your mind is an amazing thing and will figure out how to fix itself some way. It may not be the right way, but it will find a way to move forward. Many women are suffering from mental illness that has stemmed from being sexually abused. Because it's fear that dominates and how you respond to that fear is what manifests itself in different ways. Some women may have social anxiety, which makes it hard for them to function at social gatherings and in new social settings. They have fear of meeting new people because they don't know how they will be perceived. I kind of have this issue too, but I play to the fear and operate from my manic persona. Some people might have dual personalities because one personality may be the weak one that was raped and the stronger personality doesn't get raped.

Your response is normal. You may respond how I responded or how another sexual abuse victim responds. As I pointed out earlier, myself and another woman both turned to homosexuality for comfort and to exercise our sexuality. I did it for a period of time, while she made it a lifestyle. Although I was sexually abused multiple times, which made me fear and hate men. I never could totally turn to women. Sometimes I became empathetic with my abuser and remained in some type of relationship with them after the abuse.

You may have become promiscuous because that was comfortable to you. Instead of having a guy rape you again, you slept with any guy who came your way. Or you were the aggressor and sought out those guys. Your response manifested itself in low self-esteem and the need for a man's affection to become complete or validate you. Or you could have become apathetic like me. You don't equate sex with love. It's just sex. You may have been incapable of love because of your deep pain. Whichever way you responded it's okay. You are normal. Don't think anything is weird with you. *Beautiful Soul, you are very normal. Let's pray and ask God to ease your mind with how you responded to your abuse.*

Prayer

Dear Lord, help me to accept that everyone responds to their sexual abuse differently. This was mine. I am completely normal and should not be ashamed at how my behavior changed after I was sexually abused. I thank you for removing that guilt and shame off of me and out of my mind. Thank you for hearing and answering my prayer.

In Jesus' name,

Amen!

Chapter 16

Don't Rerun the Episode!

Many people, like me, replay the act over and over again. This is probably the hardest thing to stop you from doing in the first couple of months after it happened or revisiting it every now and again. We tend to try and relive the act so we can prevent it from happening again, save, erase it from our being or try to justify why it happened. I only replayed the first rape by cousin "Darryl" at fifteen over and over again for about two to three months after it happened. Then I would think about it yearly before I placed it in the back of my mind, cousin "Derrick" raped me six years later.

At that time, I didn't want to remember any of it. For me, I kept trying to figure out what I did wrong and how I could have avoided it. I also remember engraving it into my being that I was damaged! Yup, and this is why. Don't you dare think anyone will want you after this! Remember he did this to you and that happened too. Although years later I would bury it in the back of my subconscious, whenever I thought about falling in love, your damaged popped up subconsciously in my head.

I have what some would say is a personality that tends to hold on to things. I hold on to bad events, mistakes and negative thoughts. I have a hard time letting things go and moving on. I get stuck in the bad moment and keep replaying it, constantly digging at a wound and the damage to the point that it gets worse.

Although, I think I am doing myself justice. My reasoning for dwelling on the past and bad memories were to prevent myself from repeating those mistakes. It may help you not to repeat bad mistakes or situations, but in actuality it prohibits you from moving forward and focusing on positive things.

My mind was mostly consumed with negativity and very little positivity. This negativity was hindering me from the very thing I was trying to do, make fewer mistakes. I created an atmosphere of negativity around me. I dwelled in the past of my hurt and pain. I really didn't know what it felt like to live in the present and hope for the future because I kept on going back. Most of it was subconscious. I had no idea that I created my own living hell. It's one thing to assess what went wrong in your mistakes, but don't constantly speak, bash and condemn yourself through replaying the memory of your sexual abuse.

According to God's word we are to forget those things that are behind and reach for the things that are before (or ahead of us). Philippians 3:13. This was a powerful scripture for me, because I likened it to driving. You cannot drive forward while looking in the rearview mirror, can you? Nope! You would crash because you would be too focused on what is behind

you. It's over you. You got through it, you passed it, it

happened. Thinking about it over and over cannot

change and will never change the past. There is no reset

button. It's in the past, it's history. The only thing you

can do is change what is to come. Therefore your focus

should only be on what you can change.

Having this paradigm shift was extremely hard

for me, because I have operated like this for so many

years. I couldn't understand that concept. Sometimes

you have to retrain your mind to shift in your thinking

and actions. Therefore, ladies stop tormenting yourself

about what happened. You don't deserve to be

tormented over and over again. You don't deserve to be

punished with what someone else did to you. I know

you are trying to understand the why, the how, and how

to prevent it from happening again.

Constantly beating yourself up by constantly

replaying the message "I'm damaged" over and over is not helping you to acknowledge the pain, it's hurting you. You are remembering it and constantly trying to figure out where you went wrong. You are dwelling in the past of sexual abuse. This is you placing the fault on you! Remember IT'S NOT YOUR FAULT!! You are not to blame.

You need to make up in your mind that you will not replay the abuse any more. You will not dwell in mourning, but you will move on and live your life the God intended you to do. You have already acknowledged it and now you need to move forward in your healing.

Chapter 17

Forgive Them! (*Let your abuser free*)
Matt 6:12 -Forgive us our debts as we forgive our debtors

Oh NO! I have to forgive that, choice word, expletive, expletive. (cursing) I know how you feel! I felt the same way too! I said *Heck No!* Forgiveness has never been an easy task for me. I always believed in an eye for an eye. Maybe an eye for an eye, ear, leg and arm, yes I loved to get revenge on people that have done me wrong. I was good at getting people back. I wanted you to remember to never ever cross me again; crossing me was a mistake that you would regret for your entire life.

The thought about forgiving my cousin "Harold" for molesting me wasn't possible. For me, I have been carrying this since I was seven, last year was when I could actually speak his name, although I still wanted nothing to do with him. The thought of him, disgusted me. I really prayed hard for God to help me to forgive him and release him from it. I was angry, why should I let him go free without punishment, without owning up to what he did? God revealed to me that he let me go free for many things that I had done to other people, and also that this was killing me, internally.

The anger that I held onto for years was hurting me. I harbored the resentment toward him even though I didn't replay the memory, because when his name was mentioned I remembered everything and I would just suck my teeth in disgust. Yes I know that he had mental and behavioral issues too, so that could have led him to molesting me, but does that give him a pass? What about the men who didn't have behavioral issues, the men that just couldn't help themselves. Like for real God? I didn't understand God's forgiveness without recompense.

But I had to learn that this step was very necessary for healing and to help move forward. Forgiveness is major! It helps you to set yourself and the person who hurt you, free. If you have built up anger towards someone, all you are doing is poisoning yourself. You are not hurting them. Most of the time the person doesn't even remember or care about the pain they caused you. They have moved on. It didn't affect them like it affected you.

Forgiving your abuser sets you free and helps you to forget about what happened in a healthy way. It allows you to free yourself of that huge weight that you have been carrying since you were sexually abused. It removes that toxicity from your blood and your mind. Think about it, you have been carrying this anger toward this person for how long? When you forgive a person of their trespass against you, and give it to God, you no longer are judge, jury and executioner. You no longer have the job of making their life miserable, and making sure they pay for what they did to you. That's God's job.

In *Romans 12:19- Dearly beloved, avenge not yourselves, but rather give place unto wrath: for it is written, Vengeance is mine; I will repay, said the Lord.* God will do a better job repaying them, than you will. Therefore forgive your abuser, then set them and yourself free. When you forgive them you also open up your heart to receive more love, kindness and grace when the pain is released.

Think about it, this resentment has been taking up space in your heart and wasting your energy. Let it go and focus on your healing. I know you have probably heard of this before, having unforgiveness or anger/hate towards someone is like drinking poison in hopes that the other person dies or gets poisoned. But nothing happens to them, you are only poisoning yourself while they go on about their life. Let them go!

Give them over to God and let him deal with them accordingly. *Remember the law of sowing and reaping, whatsoever a man soweth, that he will reap. (Galatians 6:7)* Even if God forgives them for their sin, they will still have to reap what they've sown. It's no longer your problem; focus on your healing and becoming whole again. Don't even worry about how God will repay them. It is no longer your problem.

Now please don't misinterpret this as me saying that if you are sexually abused you shouldn't seek justice. You should definitely seek justice if the statute of limitations hasn't expired and that is what you need to assist with your closure, forgiveness process, and healing.

But for women who have long exceeded the statute of limitations and have been carrying this burden for many years or women that don't want to seek justice, it's time to release you and your abuser.

I had to see all but three of those that have sexually abused me over and over. I had to smile, greet and embraced them as if nothing happened. I protected them and kept silent about my abusers because they were family or close family friends, and I didn't want them to be looked down upon or create rifts in our family dynamic. I didn't even want them to be angry with me. Yes even after they abused me and caused me all of this pain.

Three of them actually acknowledged the sexual abuse and asked for forgiveness, which I appreciated. Although, I appreciated the sincere apology from my cousin "Darryl" that raped me, I never really forgave him at the time. I still had hatred for him, because he was able to just move on and have relationships and all I could do was shut down, unable to function properly. I think this was the same for other two as well, but this year I dug deep in my heart and forgave them all and set us all free.

Beautiful Soul,

I beg of you to set yourself free from this heavy burden and move a step closer to your permanent healing and complete restoration. Even though you cannot see it from this perspective, this will make more of impact on you than them. They will see the God in you to forgive them, maybe receive Christ, and be delivered from their sickness and sins, so they won't abuse anyone ever again. You are also cutting the ties that you had with them, once and for all. That pain inflicted on you lingered over you, dictated you and it connected you to them. They no longer have the power to hurt you, demean you, or bind you. They were the slave master to your emotions from that abuse and now that you forgave them and set yourself free, you have taken back control of your emotions.

Prayer

Dear Lord, I come to you as humbly as I can. I need your help to help me forgive my abusers. Help me to give them over to you. You be the executioner, judge and jury. You said vengeance is mine and that you will repay. Therefore you repay them for what they did to me. I release myself from this heavy burden that I have been carrying and I remove the power that this person had over me. Thank you giving me a forgiving heart where there was anger and hatred. I now allow you to fill my heart with peace. I thank you for the release.

In Jesus' name,

Amen!

Chapter 18

Forgive Others

Sometimes we are upset with a loved one, who we thought knew or should have known.

Beautiful Soul, this is another hard place! Many of us hold grudges against our loved ones and friends who didn't help us and we accuse them for allowing the abuse to happen. We try to divide this pain and burden of this sexual abuse among as many people. We hold animosity against those who should have known. How could they have not? Why didn't my older sisters care enough to look for me when I went missing? Why couldn't they tell that I was acting different, quieter or acting out?

We get angry that we are the ones that have to bear the pain while others that were around get off scot free. This is how I felt about my older sisters when I remembered the time that I was molested by cousin

"Harold". I was so angry that they didn't care enough about me to look for me. Didn't they see that I was missing for some time? Didn't they think that I would pop after a couple of minutes and tag them again? Why were they so glad that I was out of their hair? All they had to do was come in the darn room! I was right next door! They probably walked past the door while it was happening and didn't think twice about it. Why was I such a bother that they didn't think I was worth saving?

So many thoughts and questions went through my head. I also wondered why my mother would let him in our house, knowing he had mental issues. Why would they let their little daughter roam around him without making sure he was supervised? Was I that bad or annoying that when I disappeared and was quiet, everyone felt relieved? I often fought with my sisters in my teen years and I believe that the sexual abuse was one of the reasons for it. I held them guilty for not saving me. I felt abandoned by my mother and sisters and deep down in my heart I held them partially responsible.

As I came to know the Lord Jesus Christ, I realized this was not the case. I couldn't point the finger at them and secretly hold them accountable when they truly had no clue. Granted my mother knew he was troubled, which is why he came to stay with us for the winter, but she probably thought it was just behavioral and didn't think anything like that would happen.

She was always busy cleaning the house; tending to my father and her four kids, she had a lot to occupy her mind. My sisters were twelve and fourteen at the time and were probably glad that I went on to do something else. I assumed that the last thing they wanted to do was play hide and go seek or tag with their little sister. As teens, they were into boys, music and their friends and I wanted to play games that they had grown out of.

You see when you look at the situation through a forgiving lens you can understand what was going in the minds of your family members and those that were around. You can understand that they really didn't know nor did they intend to hurt you. In some circumstances where your mother or father did know, they might have not known how to handle it and were probably afraid as well.

In cases where your mother chose her boyfriend or father over you, she probably didn't know what else to do, which could have been a product of her upbringing. She may have been abused herself and didn't know how to handle it or insecure and depended upon a man and thought you would be fine. She may have thought you were too young and wouldn't remember it. I don't know. I'm just giving you another perspective.

There are so many reasons of why you didn't get the help or protection from those who were close to you, but you cannot keep this burden on them either. You have to forgive them for whatever wrong you think they've done, even for the wrong that they did do.

When I finally told my mother about my cousin "Harold" molesting me she was so sad to hear and kept apologizing over and over again, she didn't know.

She knew something was wrong with him mentally but she never thought he would do such a thing to me. She felt awful that I never told anyone, because if I had said anything, my father would have put a beating on him. Funny thing is, I knew this to be true because one of my mother's cousins, who was an adult at the time, said something inappropriate to my oldest sister when he was staying out our house. She was sixteen and my sister told my parents and my father went crazy. He beat him up, cursed him out and banned him from our house. He was not having that at all. Therefore I knew my family loved me and it was just something that went unnoticed in a busy house. I forgave my mother and sisters; I released them from what they didn't know. It wasn't their fault.

Now that you have forgiven your loved ones, call them and let them know. Give them a hug and tell them how much you love them. This is a major key to your healing. You have to acknowledge all parties to whom you held accountable and forgive them or their role in your sexual abuse. Now you are able to move forward without the heavy burdens.

I ask you now to close your eyes and say a prayer.

Prayer

Dear God, I pray that you can give me the strength to forgive those who knew about my sexual abuse and those who didn't know. I no longer hold them accountable for what happened. I pray that as you heal me of this pain, that you will also heal them because it hurt them that they couldn't or didn't stop this traumatic experience from happening to me. Lord, I know that they love me and they wouldn't purposely allow this horrible act to happen to me. If they were bound by fear, I pray that you deliver them from that spirit and give them strength to stand up against an abuser if they can prevent it the future. If they turned a blind eye, because that is what they were taught, I pray that you teach them how to respond by speaking up and interceding. Lord if they reacted in a way that only you know why, I pray that you reveal to them that it was wrong, allow them to repent unto you and then you show them the right

way to respond in case this happens again. I thank

you for giving me the power to forgive and release

them of this burden. Thank you for healing us all and

bringing us closer as family again.

In Jesus' name, I pray,

Amen!

Chapter 19

Let Love In!

Allow God to love you, despite your brokenness

Ezekiel 16:4-7, And as for thy nativity, in the day thou was born thy navel was not cut, neither was thou washed in water to supple thee; thou was not salted at all, nor swaddled at all. 5- None eye pitied thee, to do any of these unto thee; but thou was cast out in the open field, to the loathing of thy person; in the day that thou was born. And when I passed by thee, and saw the polluted in thy own blood, I said unto thee when thou was in thy blood, Live; yea I said unto thee when thou was in thy blood, Live.

This is my one of my favorite scriptures. This is the place where you'll find that despite whatever state you are in, God loves you just the way you are. He loves you despite your circumstance, what you've done, what you have been through or who you've been with. He

loves you in your brokenness. He loves you in your

ugliness. Everything that man (humankind) would look

down upon or frown at, God loves you through it all.

You are precious to Him, you are beautiful. In the above

Scripture God details how he sees us, how we are out in

the open field, bleeding out of our wounds, our pain, our

heartache, our brokenness from this sexual abuse.

When our life seems like it is over and we are left

to waste away and die. God walks past us and tells us to

LIVE. I really love the detail in this scripture, can you

imagine a baby just being born and instead of someone

giving it love and affection, they throw it out in the open

desert to rot and die. They are unprotected from

predators. It is still connected to the umbilical cord and

probably the placenta. It's not covered in any clothes or

wrapped up in any blankets with a cute little hat. No

one is swooning over this newborn baby, but it's left out

in an open field, not protected from animals that are looking for food. Just thrown out like a piece of trash. It's probably crying at the top of its lungs but its cries falls on deaf ears because no one is around to hear. And not that anyone is around to hear it; no one cares enough to listen!

There may be people around you, but no one is attentive enough to even listen to your wailing and silent screams. Just like the baby you have been discarded like trash; you are in your lowest state. You are DAMAGED! Cast to the side, left and forgotten about! This newborn baby has blood all over it from birth and no one thought enough of it to even wash him or her up! This is how I felt after my first rape by cousin "Darryl", abandoned, lonely, and discarded.

There was no one to console me, no one to hear my cries, no one to understand the gaping wound that was bleeding out profusely. I was slowly dying in my own grief and thoughts. I was broken and rejected, innocent yet filthy and some of you may feel that way too. That person man-handled you, forced your legs open and shoved themselves or an object inside of you, not caring about how much it hurt, the agony of being helpless while they thrusted themselves in and out of your lifeless body.

There were small pieces of you leaving, your consciousness eroding with each motion from them. You lie there in disgust, pain, agony, and numbness, while they ignored your reactions for the sake of their own guilty pleasures. You prayed that it would end soon. Then when it was finally over, you just laid there trying to collect yourself and whatever dignity you had left. After you've been discarded as if a horrible act didn't just happen to you, you go on in life and try to survive the best way you can.

God sees you struggling to breathe; he sees you

covered in the mess, wallowing in your own blood and broken tissue, wasting away! He sees it all and instead of looking past us like others might, He lets us know, that which looks like our end, is our beginning. He breathes life into us through His words. As you read in the text, it tells us not only did we live after this condition, but we grew and expanded, we increased instead of diminished. Our wounds were bandaged up, the bleeding stopped, and the emptiness was now filled. The abandonment replaced with love and kindness. We started to thrive again.

He then showed you more love, by covering you and making a covenant with you. He covered your scars, your nakedness (where you were exposed and vulnerable), your hurt and pain. You became His through accepting Jesus Christ as your Lord and Savior. He then thoroughly cleanses you, of all of your scars, blemishes, and stains from your past. He washes away all of the blood that you were covered in. All of the mess, He washes it away so that there is no more evidence that is was once there.

He dresses you in fine clothing, adorns you with gold and silver jewelry and places a jewel on your forehead. He feeds you; He's your provider and nourishes that which was once deprived. He picked up your pieces and took care of them by putting them back together again. He restores you to better than what you once were. Now when people see you, you are exceedingly beautiful. You are the cat's meow, whereas in times past you felt or looked low, ugly and overlooked because of your sexual abuse. You are now shining bright for the entire world to see. There's a glow about you because you are healthy, whole and loved despite what you've been through.

The beauty is that God loved you when you were in your mess, at your ugliest, when no one else loved you or could have loved you. You were in pieces and some didn't understand why. But God saw all of your pieces and that you were still attached to your abuser. The cord wasn't cut, and you weren't completely healed! You were still bleeding out of your wound which was infected and God needed to debride it and clean it out so that you could heal properly!

In Isaiah 61:3, it states that the coming and acceptance of Jesus will bring reward and redemption. *To appoint unto them that mourn in Zion, to give unto them beauty for ashes, the oil of joy for mourning, the garment of praise for the spirit of heaviness; that they might be called trees of righteousness, the planting of the LORD, that he might be glorified.*

He also wants to give you a double portion for your shame. Will you allow God to love you just as you are in all of your imperfection? This is so important! Because we are trying to fix ourselves up before we go outside in front of people or to the church. Very few people know everything about us, even our besties, boyfriends and husbands. We hold some things back because we are afraid that they might reject us because they wouldn't understand what happened or cannot fathom what we're going through and why we feel this way.

My reactions to my abuse probably weren't the most positive decisions; I didn't want anyone to know! But God knows everything! He knows everything that happened to you and everything that you did! All of the skeletons in your closet, even the things you can't remember when you were drunk or high! He sees all and knows all, and loves you anyway. (John 3:16) *he loves you so much that he sent his only begotten son, that none shall perish, but if you believe in him you shall have everlasting life.* He loves you so much that He has the patience to put all of your pieces back together again.

Allow Him to hold you and comfort you; allow Him to love you unconditionally! Yes He knows what happened to you! Yes He knows how you responded and the things that you did to mask the pain, but He is still there beckoning you to come unto Him. He's still there waiting for you to call upon Him to reveal your wounds so that He can heal it. He is still waiting for you to respond to his unwavering love and support.

Although you have shoved many away, allow Him to love you wholly without any fear. You've been toiling with this thing long enough, you've been carrying this burden long enough; you've been beating yourself down about it long enough; you have been lying to yourself that you are okay long enough; come to Him and allow him to heal you with his unconditional love.

I knew all of this because I read the bible. I listened to sermon after sermon, however for years; I wouldn't allow God to love me unconditionally. I was still in denial that I deserved it. This is why it's necessary to acknowledge your pain, and be honest with yourself.

His love is enduring and doesn't discriminate. Now that you finally understand that you are not at fault, can you allow God to show you real love? Let God show you what it's like to be loved. *Beautiful Soul, open your heart and allow God to love you just as you are.*

Do you feel His love filling and overflowing your heart? This is a place where you have to stay until you complete the next step, loving yourself. It may feel weird, but remember God is not like man. He loves us despite ourselves.

Prayer

Dear Lord, I know that you see everything; nothing is hidden from your eyes. You see me in all of my damage, pain and shame. Today I allow you to love me unconditionally. I come to you just as I am, in all of my mess. I am going to let you put me back together with your loving kindness. I will not move your hand or deny myself your love anymore. I believe that I am acceptable to receive your love. I thank you for filling my heart today.

In Jesus' name, I pray,

Amen!

Chapter 20

Love Yourself!

See yourself as God sees you without the open wounds

Now that you allowed God to love you in spite of what you've been through, now it's time for you to fall in love with yourself again. If you are like how I was, I couldn't stand myself. I acted like I loved myself a lot, so other people wouldn't treat me bad and mask my true self, but I never forgave myself for allowing all of the sexual abuse to happen.

I still saw myself as damaged even though I prayed the prayers and believed what God said concerning my life. I still didn't see myself as whole, nor love myself unconditionally. I still felt unworthy of His blessings and love. As many of us do, I am my worst critic. I critiqued everything. I set a high bar for myself.

I felt as if I had to work twice as hard as others because of what I had been through. I had to shine even brighter to cover scars.

Learning to love yourself, the good, the bad and the ugly, can be hard, especially when you have been sexually abused. Through the word of God we are able to see ourselves as God sees us. We understand that no one is sin-less or without sin. Everyone has their own past or issues that they are dealing with. But through the guidance and the power of God, the Holy Spirit, we are becoming more like Jesus every day. It's a step by step process. It's not an overnight process. You're going to have to learn to look in the mirror and like what you see.

Beautiful Soul, start speaking positive things to yourself, I tend to always point out the negative in my life and scold myself when I have done something wrong. I have now learned to affirm myself, to speak positive words to myself, even when I fall short.

I now look in the mirror and love the reflection that I see. I make it a point to fix myself up daily even if I'm not going anywhere and I take a pic of myself to remind myself of how beautiful I am. I've hated myself for so long. I spoke down to myself in my thoughts, and I had to correct that behavior and show love to myself. I wrote down a list of things that I am good at to affirm my worth, and when I am feeling down about myself, I pull it out and read it. I also focus on my gifts and talents that remind me that I am worthy. I often pull out a sketch or look at a dress that I made and it reminds me that I am somebody that is gifted and talented. Also the word of God says in Philippians 4:8

Finally, brethren, whatsoever things are true, whatsoever things are honest, whatsoever things are just, whatsoever things are pure, whatsoever things are lovely, whatsoever things are of good report; if there be any virtue, and if there be any praise, think on these things.

For those of you who think that this is a hard thing, if you don't love yourself or feel that you are unworthy to be loved, how do you think you will present yourself to other people? How can you expect to have healthy relationships? How can you expect other people to love you if you don't love yourself? You have to embrace who you are and what you been through, but understand that you are changing every day. You are growing in God's love and becoming a better you every day.

Please remember that no one's perfect! Everyone has their issues but embrace yours, acknowledge your shortcomings and ways that you will improve them. Create a plan to overcome your issues, one step or day at a time.

So Beautiful Soul what does God say about you?

How does God see you? According to Psalms 139:14, *I will praise thee; for I am fearfully and wonderfully made: marvelous are thy works; and that my soul knoweth right well.* So what does this mean? It means a couple of things. The first is that you were fearfully made to reverence God, to be in awe of God, to trust and follow him. Secondly, you were made wonderfully! Let's break down that word. In Hebrew, wonderfully means palah, which is described as distinguished or set apart. In the English dictionary wonderful means splendid, an exciting wonder, something that is amazing, beautiful and astonishing. You are a sight to behold. The masterpiece that is you is an extraordinary work of God! That God is worthy to be praised for it.

You are an amazing specimen! A beautiful creation! I want you to take a second and meditate on the aforementioned description of you. Therefore even if you cannot see anything good about yourself, think about what God says about you. Then you will start to

see the good that is really in you. You will be able to love

yourself as God loves you and you will be able to move

to the next step in your healing.

Prayer

Dear Lord, I come to you has humbly as I know how.

You are the lover of my soul, the Alpha and Omega.

You declared the things to come from the ancient of

days. Lord you can see what I can't see and you know

what I don't know. Thank you for loving me despite

myself. Thank you for seeing me as a complete whole

woman, nothing missing, nothing broken. Help me to

see myself through your eyes, complete and whole

walking in the purpose that you have predestined for

me before I was brought forth out of my mother's

womb. According to Jeremiah 1:5, Before I formed

thee in the belly I knew thee; and before thou camest

forth out of the womb I sanctified thee, and I

ordained thee a prophet unto the nations. Lord, shut

my mouth that I don't speak against your will for my

life, but I speak in accordance with it. Help me to see

the good in me that I am worthy of your love and

blessings. Help me to understand that because your love is so great, it covers my shortcomings. It heals me from my past and gives me strength to face another day. Father help me to rehearse your word concerning my life, instead of the negative words and opinions from myself. Validate me through you word! Redeem me from those that seek to put me down. I understand that you will give me the good of the land as I follow your commands through obedience. (Isaiah 1:19) Lord help me to see the beauty that you have given me for my ashes. I thank you for filling my mouth with positive words concerning me and thank you for your unwavering love!

In Jesus' name, I pray,

Amen!

Chapter 21

Heal From Your Past

It's time to completely heal. When you have allowed God to love you and then you start loving yourself you will complete your healing process. Your pain will just be a memory of something in time that happened so long ago. You no longer feel the agony or deep hurt that you once felt, because you understand the power of God's love and how it has healed your brokenness, properly healed that gaping wound, and restored you to your right self!

After you have acknowledged the pain from the abuse, the effects from the pain, you are able to move forward. You realize what you need from God to complete your healing. If you feel sensitivity when you talk about a certain event or a topic is brought up, God still needs to heal you. Weeping and sensitivity are two different things, no? When you feel yourself trying to mask the pain and bury it with an act, you still need to heal! Therefore you need to identify the pain, acknowledge it and ask the Lord for healing and strength to overcome it. But you cannot stay here; it's time to move forward.

This was just a chapter in your book, and a whole book for me. Once your healing has begun, you're embracing that yes. You had a traumatic sexual abuse experience that happened to you, but it didn't come to destroy you. You still have a life to live and to do so more abundantly. You are loveable, and you still have purpose. Stop standing in the past, it's time to see what the next step is for you now that you have healed. What is your purpose? If you haven't figured out your God given purpose, now is a great time to inquire of the Lord. What is it that he has in store for you?

You will not be defined by this sexual abuse, but

allow it to be a milestone when you thought you were broken beyond repair. When you're able to look back and even discuss the sexual abuse experience and the affects without falling apart you are healed. Instead of thinking that you are still unworthy, you start to think about living a blessed life without an outstanding debt hanging over your head. This is an amazing place that you no longer need to hide behind, mask or fear of being exposed. The scarlet letter has been removed and you are beginning to feel normal again. You can now identify your masking behavior and correct it.

The unending cycle of those memories and the pain are now dissipating. You are finally getting up from your bed of mourning and are anticipating a new day. You are thinking about the future, healthy relationships and possibly a new love if you are single. You might think about a career that you always wanted to do, but your pain and brokenness kept you from it.

Chapter 22

It's New Day!

What happened in your past doesn't dictate what you are in your future

This is something my Pastor says often after deliverance has gone forth. Today is the first day of the rest of your life. In the bible it states, that old things are passed away, {*2nd Corinthians 5:17. Therefore if any man be in Christ, he is a new creature: old things are passed away; behold, all things become new*}. When you receive Jesus Christ as your lord and savior, you are a new creation.

You are brand new! You have a clean slate. What you been through has been erased as if it didn't happen. The wound has been completely healed and it no longer needs to be tended to. The broken skin, cells, tissue and muscle have been replaced with new skin, tissue, cells and muscles. You are a new creation and your past can no longer lay claim to you or your future. It cannot hinder you or appear as a blemish on your record.

So what does this new lease on life do for you? It gives you the freedom to start again or start anew. Now you are able to find out who you are, your capabilities, and nothing is hindering your success! What did you always want to do? Who did you always want to be? What were your fantasies? What were your dreams? How did you envision yourself before the traumatic sexual abuse experience? Did you want to get married? Have children? Even if you are beyond the child bearing age, did you know that you can adopt? Or if children and marriage aren't part of your dreams, what would you like to do? Did you want to become more socialable or outgoing? Try a new career? Anything? It's your dream!! You are brand new! What would you like to achieve or accomplish?

You have a clean slate. I like to equate it to

getting your credit cleaned up. All of your bad debt has been removed from your credit report and you are given a true fresh start, you don't have to wait seven years for the bankruptcy to come off of your credit.

Take a minute and dare to dream without limits! Smile and laugh while you think about your new amazing life! Envision yourself walking it out, living in joy every day, waking up to your cute hubby, seeing your kids bust through or bang on your door, waking you up before you are ready (this is my fantasy)! You can imagine yourself living out the career you've always wanted, having the peace and the reassurance of who you are!

Imagine your life without being drunk, high or any other type of self-medication. Imagine living without fear! This is my testimony; the memories from my traumatic sexual abuse left me in such a petrified state. I would get so far and the fear of my past would creep up and serve as a reminder as to why my dreams were unattainable. It whispered in my ear, *you can't do this, you are weak, and you are broken. If you try to do this or that, I will come out and expose who you are really are.* It was paralyzing. Allowing God to heal and restore me set me free from the spirit of fear. Just like I was set free, you have been too! I challenge you to choose a small dream or fantasy, and plan it out. What do you see yourself doing now that you have been reborn, repaired and restored?

This is an important stage in your process of restoration. You have to envision yourself living your dream before you are able to walk in it. This is liberation from the burden you have been carrying. Let's dwell on your dreams for a moment. If you wanted to get married, what kind of guy do you see yourself marrying? Where would you live? What kind of social life would you have? How would you dress, now that you've been given a fresh start? For me, I was so torn with my choices of clothing. On one hand I loved my shape, but on the other hand I loathed it because I thought it was the cause of my many sexual abuse experiences. Now I don't think about as much, and I wear what I feel comfortable in. I am now in my late thirties, and I'm happy that my breasts still look a little perky in some deep cut blouses! "Yippee." I don't feel dirty when I wear revealing clothing. Although, I like to leave some things to the imagination.

But for the first time in a long time, I love me and everything that pertains to me. I love my shape and the way I fill out clothes. I even gained some weight and I love the way I look overall when I get dressed. This is such a great feeling. Some days I feel like jumping for joy, like the actors in the commercial. I'm enjoying my new free life. I want you to make a list of all of the things you ever wanted to do. Don't worry how long or short the list will be this is to help you imagine your new day!

I want you to really experience this newness!

Prayer

Dear Lord, Help me to see myself as new, give me the strength to move forward in this newness. Destroy the spirit of fear that may cause me withdraw and go back. God reveal to me your purpose for my life. Show me where I fit in the body of Christ. Bring back to my remembrance all of the amazing things you spoke and promised me before the sexual abuse occurred. Completely remove the blinders that the sexual abuse caused so I can see myself living the zoe kind of life that you designed for me. Thank you for completely healing me from the effects of my sexual abuse.

In Jesus' name, I pray

Amen!

Chapter 23

A New You!

Start to walk in your newness

Now that have envisioned your new you, it's time for you to start walking in it. This was an extremely hard thing for me to do. As I stated in the previous chapter, I would envision a new me, goal or task; then fear would whisper in my ear and remind me of my past and my scars. For a long time it was hard for me to see myself with a new day, a fresh start, and allowing people to know my deep dark secrets and not be ashamed of it because God healed me. Sometimes part of the damage would still be there hiding beneath the surface and you are not fully restored until you can walk in your newness.

When you start walking in your newness, not only did you see it and speak it, but you now believe it!

You believe and understand that you have been made new, that you are able to actually walk in it! You are able to move and operate in this new you! Your past has no more control over you! This is the manifestation of your liberty and demonstration of your belief. In *James 2:17, Even so faith, if it hath not work, is dead, being alone. {Read James 2:15-20 for context}*

Therefore what it is saying is that you can believe but if you don't act based on what you believe, it means nothing to just believe in something if you don't act on it. (what happened here? It seems like you just added my comments in the regular text.) on it. Your actions are really based on your beliefs, if you believe you can do a certain task, and then you will try until you succeed. However, if you don't believe that you can accomplish a certain task or goal, you won't even try or you may try but it's not a sincere effort. Because in the back of your mind you don't actually believe you can successfully accomplish the task, make sense right?

I want you to think about some things in your past, goals or dreams that you had in your mind, but you never accomplished because of your beliefs. Now you may say to yourself or even me, Dianne I really did believe but it didn't work out, yadda, yadda, yadda. I had to ask myself this question and when I really looked at what I believed at the time, I tried to start my clothing line or other projects. I noticed that I never really believed that I could accomplish the goal. I had so many reservations in that back of mind and deep in my heart.

Now you are starting to see how this traumatic sexual abuse experience really affected you, your beliefs and your goals. This was an Aha moment for me, although I heard God's promises, I saw that I had great talent. I was smart, and even possessed the ability to sell ice to an Eskimo. There was this underlying unworthiness and brokenness that I internalized and really believed. Therefore I acted according to my beliefs. I procrastinated when I had a project to complete because I was firm in my beliefs, I was apprehensive with a lot of my projects. I made excuses of why I couldn't focus or complete a project. I tried to blame other people, or make an excuse and say that the goal was too big. I also set myself up for failure.

I made goals that were too big and only gave myself an unrealistic amount of time to complete it and when I failed to meet my accomplished goal, I fell into the cycle of anxiety and depression. This also activated my bi-polar disorder. All the while not realizing my beliefs were off because of how I viewed myself after my traumatic sexual abuse experiences. Wow, right? My sexual abuse skewed my perception of myself. Do you see why allowing God to love you and loving yourself is so important? Also please keep in mind; I had multiple traumatic experiences so they compounded those negative thoughts on the other ones; driving me to such a low place mentally and emotionally.

Walking in your newness affirms that you actually believed that God delivered you from your past, and that you have been given a clean slate and you are actually NEW! You no longer operate in that brokenness that you have become accustomed to. Remember you had to adjust to that, because you needed to repair yourself and move on the best way you could. This is a major adjustment.

This is why in the previous chapter I spoke in depth about seeing yourself in your new liberated state. Remember I stated brokenness became so comfortable; I had lived in it since I was seven years old. All I knew was to bury and mask, internalize, internalize, internalize! I totally forgot that I was broken.

Now I had to learn how to operate again. It's like

a newborn baby learning how to walk. It's a step by step process. First you crawl, and then after you get crawling down, you start to stand up, balancing yourself on your new legs. Then after you have learned how to balance on your legs, you start taking one step at a time, moving forward in your newness.

So you ask, Dianne, how do I learn to crawl now that I finally believe that I am new? I finally replaced all of those old thoughts of abandonment, pain, rejection, hopelessness, worthless, brokenness with love, being nurtured, being tended to, worthy, hope and restoration. This is huge; this is the foundation of your faith. You speak to yourself in your mind differently. Instead of disgust and loathing, there's an admiration, there's gentleness and kindness. Through your dialogue with yourself, your perception of yourself changes. It's softer, more endearing, and you are no longer at war with yourself. Now that you are in agreement with yourself and what God sees and says about you, you can start believing his promises, thoughts and what He says you can do and have now that you are NEW! Just like a baby, your mind believes that you can move toward your goal. I would like to expand on the steps on learning how to walk in your newness. As I mentioned before a baby goes through 3 stages, crawling, standing, and walking.

<u>Crawling:</u>

So what does crawling entail? It's the first type of mobility the baby makes to get from one place to another. It's a precursor to walking. The foundation of your belief is built and you may not have huge strides, but you are moving toward your goal. They may be small and you may have to drag yourself from spot to spot but you are moving, and are not stagnant just thinking about how it would be to be in that imagined place. These are the small goals, like small milestones that show you do believe that you are new. For instance with me, I wanted to start a clothing and fashion boutique. I tried to jump out there and start walking by creating very expensive detailed collections when I didn't have the budget to finance it.

My dad always told me that I have to crawl before I walk, over and over. I would always start at the top of my goals. Super wrong. Crawling would be sketching and thinking about how I would like to enter the fashion industry based on what I have today. Start off with a smaller more inexpensive collection, something manageable with an achievable deadline. Therefore crawling is making small achievable goals to accomplish now, that will feed into your bigger goal.

Once you are able to start doing and accomplishing these small goals, you are now coupling your faith (belief) with works. In order to have faith you have to have works that support your faith or your faith is dead. You believe you can do XYZ because of your newness, and you are actually doing XYZ which is part of the bigger goal.

I want you to go back to the previous chapter where you had to make a list of what you wanted to do, now that you are new. Choose one of the most important goals to you. Now that you have chosen that goal, let's think of a few smaller goals that you set for yourself that are achievable in a short amount of time and using all of the tools that you have at your disposal.

It's your goal, nothing is stupid or insignificant. This is what makes you happy! Remember we are in a no judgement zone. Choose three to five smaller goals that you can work on now, that will assist you in reaching that bigger goal. It could be weight loss, a new wardrobe, a new career, or a hobby that you've always wanted to do.

Let's choose a new wardrobe for an example. For me, my smaller goal was to become a motivational speaker, therefore; I wanted a new wardrobe to go with that new career. I thought about how a motivational speaker would dress. What would be empowering to other women if they were to see me at an event? How can I encourage women with what I wore and also walk in my newness? I decided on a sexy classic look. This was me owning my sexuality without being in fear. I wanted to wear some fitted clothing that showcased my amazing shape and highlighted my best assets, my legs (to me anyway).

I started to implement affordable versatile pieces that I could mix and match, my actual goal was to have an event wardrobe where I could have a good amount of outfits to wear when I was called to speak. Since I can sew, this was a benefit because it tied into another goal of mine of having a successful clothing line.

I searched for really nice shoes that were discounted, but had that wow factor. I put outfits together at home in my downtime and dressed up in them. I would take pictures and envisioned myself on a podium speaking somewhere empowering women. At that point, I was activating my faith that I could achieve this goal and crawl in it.

Standing up:

Now that I have given you an understanding of what the crawling stage is, let's move on to standing and balancing. This is a crucial step because before you are able to walk in that new goal, you have to be able to stand! How do you stand? How does one balance themselves in their belief? When do you know that you are standing? These are some questions that I had for myself, since I'm always used to skipping these stages and trying to walk. I had to ponder on what this meant to me.

Standing would be affirming yourself in your belief after you have made some movement toward your goal with crawling. Since this is real life everything will not go your way! Let me repeat, everything will not go your way! You will have obstacles like all goals do. Some obstacles may be small, some may be big but you have to be able to STAND despite them both! If you are not firm in your belief this will cause you to waiver, become unstable and then fall. If you cannot balance yourself enough to stand then you definitely won't be able to get far when you try to walk.

So how do you balance yourself and become firm in your beliefs to be able to stand? Your belief in yourself has to be able to literally weather the storms that may come. While you are crawling, you are strengthening your self-esteem in this new you and new goal. Through achieving those small goals, seeing yourself achieving the big goal and reaffirming yourself through God's word and positive affirmations are going to help you stand and balance yourself.

In addition to this, I would create a small support system, just like a baby has a cheering section encouraging him or her to stand, so should you. Surround yourself with people that know what goals you are trying to achieve, and will cheer you on when you embark on a new task or put together a plan to achieve your big goal. Your support system will also encourage you and cheer you on as you take steps in achieving those goals.

Assess your gifts, talents and abilities that will help you achieve those goals. Remind yourself daily that you are able to accomplish this goal. Shut down fear and negativity with God's word. For me, I created a vision statement and my purpose of why I wanted to achieve that goal. I also remind myself that I cannot give up and give in because I want to help people. There are women out there that are just like me, having a hard time acknowledging their past hurt and are living broken lives. I look at what God has done for my life and my pain was to help others heal. I remind myself that I am capable of being a motivational speaker because of my ability to speak to anyone, anywhere, especially if I am passionate about it. I can talk for hours. I am very personable.

I have helped my friends through various situations. I can do this. When fear arises to say that people will judge me and I will be ashamed again, I recite God's word to combat that fear. After experiencing some setbacks, negative opinions and fearful thoughts and overcoming them through the various methods mentioned above, I show myself that I am able to overcome whatever comes my way. I balance and stabilize myself in this belief that I can and will achieve my goal. *Whooo Hooo I'm Standing!* Now I'm ready to walk!

It's time to walk:

It's more of a mental exercise than anything. Of course accomplishing smaller goals definitely helps, but it strengthens your belief that you can do this. And no matter what comes your way you are going to achieve your goal. It's time to tackle that big goal! You've imagined yourself walking in this "new you" goal. You wrote small plans, you have the wardrobe and attitude, your thoughts and your speech are in agreement with this new you! Walk in it! Make another plan of how you will achieve this goal. Give yourself steps!

Since your belief and faith have been solidified by your previous actions, you are now confident in each step. You may be a little wobbly because you have never done this before, but just like a baby taking steps for the first time you are elated! You are doing it! You are actually in that new career! You are wearing the new hair cut that you've always wanted, you are CONFIDENT! Real confidence! Not the façade that you have lived in since your traumatic sexual abuse experience.

You're not wearing a mask this time, it's really you! You have planned out all of the steps and you are actually doing them, not halfhearted, but fully convicted that you can do this. Now you might have some shaky nerves because this is new for you! You haven't felt this confident in a long time! It may take some time getting used to, but I believe you will get comfortable with this new you and walk soon. Your thoughts are different with every step, you hear yourself saying, "Yes I can and it will work out," rather than I don't know. Are you sure? Is this you God? Oh Lord what am I doing or I can't do this!

Your speech has changed because your beliefs

have changed. You are more stable and comfortable when you have to stand as you weather storms. You don't cave or fall down or become overwhelmed and sink. You ride the wave but maintain your posture. This newness is wonderful. Look at you, you look fabulous in that very thing you thought you couldn't do because of your brokenness. This new you is amazing! You followed through, you are not working yourself too hard, but you are pacing yourself. You are not falling back into your old habits, they are long gone. The cycle is finally broken and you are actually living the life that you actually dreamed, nothing is out of reach for you! You are finally healed and whole.

Take a step in your future, set the time, place, goal, and date that you want to achieve it. Believe it! Beautiful Soul you are on your way!

Prayer

Dear Lord, thank you for helping me see myself as you see me. Thank you for giving me more understanding of how my faith works. I believe your word concerning my life and what I want to achieve. I thank you for showing me that my belief grows in stages. Help me not to get too excited and jump out before the next step by walking before I am able to crawl. Continue to guide me in this newness that you have provided for me. I am so grateful for this second chance to achieve all of the things that I thought were impossible. You are a loving and powerful God who gives me strength to stand whenever opposition comes my way. I declare and decree that you are able to do exceedingly abundantly above all that I ask and or think according to your word in Ephesians 3:21. I also know that when I am weak in you I am made strong. Thank you for ordering my steps in this new journey.

In Jesus' name, I pray

Amen!

Chapter 24

I Am Ready For Love!

Allow yourself to be loved and give love in a new relationship

Now that you have learned to love yourself again, you see yourself as healed and whole; and you are walking in your newness and God-given purpose. You are ready to love again. As I said previously, you cannot love someone else or expect yourself to be loved properly when you don't even love, let alone like yourself. When you have insecurities, you're in pieces and you don't think that you are worth anything. You will not be able to function in a good relationship properly. You will always see yourself as unworthy of this person's love or you will give this person the task of healing you.

I believe no one can heal you from this pain even if they are a loving person. You had deep seated issues that this person had no clue of, and some issues you aren't aware of until you start peeling back the layers. You have to become whole on your own with God's help, because if that relationship doesn't work out, who will then validate you? You will become dependent on that person and that can cause a different set of issues. Your worth cannot be defined by someone else! You have to know your worth before you go into a relationship or you will bring in host of issues on top of trying to get to know and coexist with someone else.

This is something that I am passionate about. You have to know you and be comfortable with you, before you even try to start a relationship. Trust me I know! I have also seen it before with other people and it always ended in a break up.

So Beautiful Soul, now that you know whose (meaning God's child) who you are, you know what to expect, you set the expectations for how your significant other should treat you! Remember no one can walk all over you, unless you lay there and let them. You have the power to choose to accept how they treat you. You are new honey and priceless!! Your stock just skyrocketed and you are a cat's meow! If this person can't see your greatness, walk away because there are more waiting for the chance to get your attention. It's so important to believe that you are new, so you can walk in your newness, become confident in that newness so you can date with confidence. I cannot reiterate that you are new too much because out of that belief is how you will operate.

It's time to open your heart again to the idea of love! You have been healed and made whole; you have been properly repaired and restored. You don't have to be afraid of letting someone in again because the last person was probably your abuser. Or you never had the opportunity to let someone in because your traumatic sexual abuse experience damaged you to the point of creating and fortifying a wall around your heart. You are a new person and you understand that what happened happened; it is now in your past. Yes, you might be a little cautious about a new love, but you can now move forward without fear.

Some of you might be in a loving relationship, but I need to ask you are you really happy? Is this the person that you truly desired to be with? Or have you settled because of your low-self-worth and fear of rejection. See I did lower my standards at times and settled because I wanted to be in a relationship. Now this was very few, because I have a low tolerance for guys that do not peak my interest. Like I said previously, if I don't like you, I cannot fake it. I'd rather be alone than to waste my time and energy with someone that didn't satisfy me just to say that I was in a relationship. Some of you might really like or be in love with the person you are dating, but I need for you to be honest with yourself, could this relationship be better? Now that you have uncovered some deep wounds from your sexual abuse and are whole again.

Can you see how the change in you might change the relationship for better or worse? I'm not the author on all relationships but I do know that you cannot truly love another if you don't love yourself. I also believe that no man or woman can complete one another. When you enter into a relationship or marriage, it should be a whole person connecting with a whole person. You should complement each other not complete each other.

I want you to challenge yourself and think about actually falling in love. Truly in love, with no fear or apprehension, think about your dream guy. What does he look like, his features that attract you to him? Think about the way he talks, his mannerisms. What did you always desire in a man before you were sexually abused? Allow yourself to envision it so you can be more comfortable when you actually start dating.

For me, I didn't have a specific type per se, but I loved a guy with a cool laid back personality, a deep speaking voice, Brooklyn or Northern accent, enough hair on his head that I could run my fingers through it, and a great sense of humor since I love to laugh. He had to be ambitious with a lot of drive, caring because I love very hard, a nice smile and a brain! Oh, how I love a guy that is smart!

Take some time to write down your dream guy. You don't have to stick to this ideal image, but this will allow you to start seeing yourself dating with purpose again. Even though, I mentioned a lot of characteristics that I want in a man, I narrowed it down to six non-negotiables. Here's what's important to me:

1. He has to be saved and have a relationship with

God.

2. Have a thin to athletic build. He has to like to go to the gym a couple of times a week or have a desire to be healthy where we can work out and pursue our health goals together.

3. He has to be able to feed my mentality. I'm very inquisitive and I love to learn. A guy that possesses a lot of knowledge can teach me a thing or two and a great conversationalist. I love to talk about various topics, so we can move through topics easily because of his vast knowledge.

4. He has to be a leader, ambitious and a go getter. I am a super Alpha Female and will walk all over a guy if he's not strong enough to take control of the situation and tell me that he has this. I have to trust that he is capable of leading me or I won't feel secure and will become disinterested.

5. He has to possess a big heart! I love to give and help people. I cannot be with a guy who is selfish; we would constantly be at war with each other.

6. I know I have a lot. He has to have a great sense of humor. I love to laugh and I am super silly! Therefore he has to be able to make me and laugh and laugh with me about any and everything.

Just like I did above, I want you to write down your four to six non-negotiables. These are things that you need to have in a man that you are dating. If they don't possess all of these qualities, don't waste your time with them. This will also help you to think about what kind of guy you can trust and what makes you feel comfortable. Is this the guy that you can share your past with? Can you let down your guard and remove the wall with this guy? If you have been turned off from men because of your traumatic sexual abuse experience and fear of a man hurting you again, is this the guy that you can yield control to?

I know this may be extremely hard to even think about let alone do, but it's necessary to start moving forward to allow yourself to love again. Question to the ladies that have become homosexuals, now that you have been set free from your fear of men, would you start dating men again? Could you? Do you want to? If not, ask yourself what's holding you back?

As I stated in a previous chapter, my issues were fear of rejection and trust. I needed to be in control of everything and I wanted to choose who I slept with and who I didn't. I dictated the length of the relationship. I was always detached, even when I had my whirlwind romance in 2002, I still couldn't allow myself to fall completely in love. I still held a lot of my feelings and emotions back. He knew just how much I wanted him to know. He loved me beyond all of my faults that he knew of.

Yet I still wasn't able to reveal everything. It was the first time I actually thought I could get married and become a wife. The possibility of deep love scared the heck out of me! Although the relationship ended, I was given a seed of hope that I could actually become married. I could see myself in a long-term relationship where I didn't feel trapped. I am capable of loving and being loved. I believed my lie about being damaged for so long that I had to go through an experience for me to actually believe that it was possible for me. I never told him about my sexual abuse past because I wasn't healed by God yet. Therefore, I understand how you might feel being hesitant going into a new relationship with hopes of actually falling in love, and being loved, without being controlling.

I want to you also think about what has held you back from falling in love before and having a healthy relationship with a man. What excuses did you make, were you detached or too needy? Did you purposely date the opposite sex or someone that you did not desire? Did you settle for less then became uninterested because they weren't actually what you wanted? Did you create high standards for the man to meet and if he didn't meet them you discarded him quickly?

I used to do this a lot and this is another form of control and excuses as to why they don't meet your expectations. Now that you have identified what kept you from love or having a healthy relationship. The underlying feeling is fear! Let us think about how God's word combats that thinking and behavior.

(1 Timothy 1:7) *God has not given you the spirit of fear, but power, love and a sound mind.* Now that you are set free from the fear of being abused and hurt. It no longer has power over you. It no longer dictates you. The power of love is an amazing thing. According to 1 John 4:18, *There is no fear in love; but perfect love casteth out*

fear: because fear hath torment. He that feareth is not made perfect in love. It states that there is no fear in love! Yes there is no fear in love. When you are properly loved you don't have to live in fear. God makes you perfect in love, when you accept Jesus Christ as your Lord and Savior. And God leads you to the person that you are to fall in love with.

We can also use this scripture to show you what real love is. When someone really loves you that person has your best interest in mind. You can relax and let your guard down, because you don't believe that person will hurt you. They are not going to use you, nor are they looking to use you, cheat on you or abuse you. They are going to do right by you. Therefore you are in a safe place. Love brings the security that allows you to be free to give and receive love.

You are able to place your trust in that person. You see that when you don't trust that person, you won't be relaxed and you cannot relax because the fear of being hurt is tormenting you. Love is an action word. It shows you what it is. In 1 Corinthians 13-4, it details what love is. In the scripture it calls love charity. *Charity suffereth long, and is kind; charity envieth not; charity vaunteth not itself, is not puffed up.* Love is patient, love is kind, and it's unselfish. God shows us what true love is; therefore you are able to detect real love from someone.

For sexual abuse victims, we have suffered in fear for so long that we don't really understand love. Now that we have allowed God to love us and we have learned to love ourselves. We can now identify love from a guy.

There were two guys that I dated that allowed me to let most of my guard down. The action of their affection displayed these characteristics and provided me a secure environment for me to feel safe to love back. This is what you need, a safe environment that love provides.

If you are feeling fearful, ask yourself why? Does it stem from something internally or is this guy providing you a safe environment to give love? Put your trust in God, that he will lead you to the guy that will love you, like He loves you.

Sex is not Love

We cannot talk about love without talking about sex. Especially for a sexually abused victim, this was a hard concept for me to grasp. For so long, sex was a major part of my relationships because I always felt this was what men wanted from me. Even after being celibate for over eight years. I went back to what I was used to, when dating, guys lusted after me so bad so I had to give him what he wanted before he tried to take it. I also went back to what was comfortable for me.

You shouldn't have sex to fall in love. You should fall in love because you love that guy, and you want to have sex, or in our case since we are now in Christ Jesus, you want to have sex with your husband. It's the act that binds you together, when the two shall become one. I'm not going to go too much in depth on this topic because that is a book in itself. Being a victim of sexual abuse, you tend to think that that is all you are and where your worth lies. But it's not, you are so much more than what is between your legs and you have so much to offer.

Sex should be saved for your husband because when you have sex before you are married it creates false emotions that are based on sex, especially if the sexual experience is a good one. When your souls become intertwined after the sexual act, you long for this person in a way that mimics love. Instead, it's just that you have become one with this guy and that attachment is extremely strong. The more you engage in sexual activity with this guy, the stronger the bond will become. When you finally notice that your important needs aren't being met or satisfied, you have a hard time disconnecting with that person.

It actually rips you apart when you finally end the relationship. It's called a soul tie. This is why you might have stayed with your abuser or in a dysfunctional relationship in the past. I would say stay away from men that are only talking about sex; they already told you what they are interested in. To me this is the last thing you need. Sex doesn't define you!

After the thrill is gone from sex, you can still communicate, you still want to see this man happy and vice versa. You both get excited when you see each other or speak to each other. You want to enjoy life with this person. This is the love that you want! When you are in love with someone, the selfish human nature takes a back seat and it's more about a mutual partnership where both of you are reaping the benefits.

Now this is not going to be an overnight process. Getting to this stage and engaging in healthy dating will lead to a healthy relationship and hopefully, if it's God's will and your will, a healthy marriage.

As it relates to dating, I wouldn't advise you to bring up your past sexual abuse on the first or second date, but if you are getting closer to this person and are thinking about becoming intimate, I think you should let them know. You can casually date until someone comes along that makes you want to cut the rest off, but allow yourself to have fun and date! Daydream about love and being loved unconditionally!! Imagine yourself falling without reservations. There is someone out there that will love you like you deserve to be loved. They won't care about your past so you shouldn't either. It's not a deal breaker. Remember honey you are NEW!

Prayer

Lord, please lead, guide and direct me as I start dating again. Block any man from me who only wants to cause me pain and heartache. Remove any man from my path that comes to distract me from your purpose and destiny. And any man that only sees me as a sexual object. Open my eyes and heighten my discernment that I may see the red flags from afar before I open up my heart again. I pray that you will give me the courage to be vulnerable again, If I became guarded because I was sexually abused by my former boyfriend or a man I was dating. I pray that through your love you will block the spirit of fear that will cause me to draw away from a potential suitor that you send to me. I pray that you make his heart sensitive to my needs and give him patience to wait until I am able to give love as he desires. Also show him how to love and show me love like you love to remove any fear and provide with the security I need to trust again.

In Jesus' name,
Amen!

Chapter 25
Help Others!

Now that you have overcome your sexual abuse, help others to overcome theirs. Share with them what you learned about your own sexual abuse and how it affected you. Be open to listen to another sexual abuse victim's story. Understand that you are to be an objective listener, and allow them to vent to you their thoughts and feelings about what happened to them. Share your testimony, my testimony and how we both overcame our past and now live a new life.

This may have been the first time you have had to face your past about your sexual abuse. It could have been many years since the incident and you are now uncovering an infected wound. I know this process was hard, but it was worth it. Aren't you glad that you didn't believe the report that you were given? Aren't you happy that there was hope after what happened to you? Do you see how your sexual abuse affected your behavior and way of thinking? Were you able to have a heart to heart with yourself, shed tears and look forward to a new life without the blemish that plagued you since the sexual abuse took place?

Since I have finally opened up about my sexual abuse past, I have been an ear to other women who just like me kept it a secret for years. Women that I have known for over twenty years shared their story with me and they were able to see how their sexual abuse played a major part in the decisions that they have made. They noticed what triggered their addiction, bi-polar disorder, desire for attention and validation. They noticed some habits that they created, were ways to cope with their sexual abuse and function the best way they could.

I then realized how important it was to share my

story and I want you to know how important it is to share your story. I was able to get a lot of insight about my behavior and how I responded to my sexual abuse through God. I still have yet to attend therapy, but I hope to go soon because I want to be able to share my story of healing and redemption with other sexual abuse victims and understand how it has affected their lives as well.

Therefore I encourage you to share your story, share my story and how we both overcame this traumatic experience. Let others know what you went through physically and emotionally, because so many women have been sexually abused. Statistics state that 1-6 women have been sexually abused. Imagine how many women are going through life in a dysfunctional way. They are broken and have bandaged up themselves the best way they can. They live day to day in the shadow of their sexual abuse. Some women have over came through therapy, some overcame with God. For me God was the only way to go because it was so deep seeded that I forgot about it. I pushed it down so deep and covered my emotions with so many lies that I believed them and God had to reveal to me that I was NOT okay.

Start to share this with your family, if you never told them. Now is a good time. Let them know what happened to you, how it made you feel and the effects of that abuse. Share this with your significant other if you have one, it's time that they know when they touch you why you respond the way you did. Share your testimony about how damaged you were and how God restored you as well!!!! Help another woman that is trapped and doesn't even know it.

Prayer

Dear Lord, I thank you for healing me and making me whole. I thank you that the damage that was caused by my sexual abuse has been repaired and I have been restored to greater than what I was. I thank you for a testimony to share with others your loving grace and mercy!!! Please lead and guide me to share my story with the woman that is still bound by her past. The woman that is crying out in the open field, bleeding out of her wounds, the one that no one hears. Let her screams and cries fall on my ears so I can share with her the good news of Jesus Christ. That Jesus is able to heal her and love her back to her rightful place. Lord give me the word in my mouth that she needs to hear so she too can be healed like I was healed.

I thank you for hearing my humble prayer!

In Jesus' name, I pray,

Amen!

Love Letter

Dear Beautiful Soul,

Thank you for sharing in part of my testimony. It has been one heck of a journey. I have never been so transparent in my life. As I mentioned in a previous chapter, I am a very private person. I do not show my vulnerability at all. There hasn't been one person that I have been completely naked in front of. In this book, I held back nothing. I showed you what lied beyond my mask that I covered with for so many years, that it became my identity.

God has truly blessed me with the strength and peace to share this with you!! As well as take you through my steps toward complete healing! I am so excited about what God has done in my life and I am so excited about your complete healing and restoration! I know that God has an amazing life for you! Even though you were tagged as damaged goods and given a date of

destruction, know that you were not damaged beyond

repair.

Sincerely,

Dianne M. Dobson

ABOUT THE AUTHOR

Dianne M. Dobson is a single mother of an amazing 21 year old daughter. She was licensed as an Evangelist in 2007 and a member of New Jerusalem Temple of the Living God since 2003. She has led many to Christ Jesus and deliverance from various bondages through the word of God and the power of the Holy Spirit. In 2009, Dianne wrote and designed 6 pamphlets to assist new Christians in their walk with Jesus. These pamphlets are currently pending publishing for national and international distribution.

Dianne graduated from the Art Institute of Philadelphia with a degree in Fashion Design in 2010. In March 2012, she launched her own clothing line D.I. and online boutique, www.d-i-boutique.com in 2014. Her clothing line is geared toward the women of influence, which includes high end custom clothing. In 2017 she plans to launch her non-profit company for young ladies to empower them to become successful whole women.

Contact for Booking, Comments and Testimonies

diinternationalbusiness@gmail.com

ACKNOWLEDGMENTS

I would first like to thank God for giving me the strength to overcome my traumatic sexual abuse experiences, the courage to write about them and share them with the world. This was not an easy thing to do. I thank God for the gift of writing so I can share my story in a way that people can relate. The boldness to look my abusers and shamers in the face to let them know that this has not broken me to the point I was unable to be repaired. I want to acknowledge those whose contributions to this book made it what it is today. My daughter for encouraging me to write and the reason to keep on living despite how heavy and deep, the pain was. My Pastor, Apostle Sharon R. Robinson for loving me and showing me how to follow Christ. Your words of wisdom and correction have really helped me to see myself through God's eyes! My editor Tracy, thank you for taking this book and structuring it where it was digestible to the reader. My proofreader, Lenora, thank you for reviewing and revising as needed to help me convey my story in the way that God directed me. To Arrington, my graphic designer for creating my gold restored vase!!! You made this from scratch! You did what most people said couldn't be done! My cover wouldn't be what it was without that vase!! Lastly, to all of my friends and family that have showed me undying support through this year. This was a very trying year and without you, I don't know how I would have made it!! I love you all!!!

XOXO's

Dianne

2

www.ingramcontent.com/pod-product-compliance
Lightning Source LLC
Chambersburg PA
CBHW021221090426
42740CB00006B/324